The Real War on Women

ISBN-13: 978-1537304007
ISBN-10: 1537304003

There should be "...some form of Punishment." – Donald Trump, Republican Presidential candidate after being asked if women should be punished for having abortions.

"The unborn person doesn't have constitutional rights." – Hilary Clinton. Democratic Presidential Candidate after being asked about the unborn child.

Table of Contents

1

Feminism in early America

The real *War on Women!* What does it mean? Has America declared war on women? Is it a literal war? Are there any casualties in this war? Where are the battle fields if this is a war? This is a critical look at the "Pro-choice" and "Pro-life" movements in America that I hope will clear up any fallacies that rhetoric on both sides of this issue will spew forth in an attempt to gain the upper hand politically.

Since the term *War on Women* was coined to describe a certain political party's stand on the topic of abortion we should take a brief look at where the political parties stand on the issue in general. Before the historic 1973 *Roe V. Wade* Supreme Court case that legalized abortion on demand for any reason in all States abortion was legal in certain states for certain reasons. Including a) rape or incest, b) A threat to the life of the mother, or c) In the first trimester for any reason. There were other reasons but, essentially, those were the main ones.

Abortion was legal in some states before 1900 but by 1900 it became a felony in all states. As the century wore on, however, the abortion laws changed for each state until 1973 when all laws restricting abortion were struck down by the supreme court.

One of the most interesting aspects of abortion laws before 1900 is the people who supported them. Mostly Physicians and feminists...that's right, feminists, though you won't read about any of this in today's media. It is almost a reversal of that today. Just like before 1964, most people viewed Civil Rights as a Republican thing whereas the Democrats were those who generally opposed Civil Rights legislation. But since the Civil Rights act of 1964 that reversed (2) and now the Democrats are viewed as the party of Civil Rights while the Republicans are seen as being opposed or neutral on the issue (I could go on about that, but that's a topic for a different book.)

Since the Abortion issue is generally regarded as a feminist issue let's take a look at what the Feminist movement said about abortion before 1900:

"There must be a remedy for such a crying evil as this. But where shall it be found, at least begin, if not in the complete enfranchisement and elevation of women?" – *Elizabeth Cady Stanton*

"Here we find that a husband has been procuring **poison for his wife and prospective offspring!** Not with any wish to kill the wife perhaps, but as the chances are 5 to 1 against every woman who attempts **abortion,** he could not fail to realize the danger. Had this scheme been successful in destroying only the life aimed at, what could've been the man's crime – and what should be his punishment if, **as accessory to one murder he commits two?"** – *Sarah F. Norton* (after a man fed his wife an abortifacient and she died as well as the child.)

"... **Wives deliberately permit themselves to become pregnant of children and then, to prevent becoming mothers, as deliberately murder them while yet in their wombs.** Can there be a more demoralized condition than this? ... We are aware that many women attempt to excuse themselves for procuring abortions, upon the ground that it is not murder. But the fact of resort to so weak an argument only shows the more palpably that they fully realize the enormity of the crime." – *Victoria Woodhull.* (The first woman to declare a bid for the Presidency.)

"When a man steals to satisfy hunger, we may safely conclude that there is something wrong in society – **so when a woman destroys the life of her unborn child,** it is an evidence that either by education or circumstances she has been greatly wronged." – *Maddie H. Brinckerhoff*

"The gross perversion and destruction of motherhood by the abortionist filled me with indignation, and awakened active antagonism. That the honorable term 'female physician' should be exclusively applied to those women who carried on this shocking trade seemed to me a horror. It was an utter degradation of what might and should become a noble position for women." – *Dr. Elizabeth Blackwell*, who was the first woman to earn a medical degree, referring to abortionist *Madame Restell* of New York.

"Guilty? Yes, no matter what the motive, love of ease, or desire to save from suffering the unborn innocent, the woman is awfully guilty who commits the deed. It will burden her conscience in life, it will burden her soul in death; but oh! Thrice guilty is he who, for selfish gratification, heedless of her prayers, indifferent to her fate, drove her to the desperation which impels her to the crime." – *Susan B. Anthony* (though there is some controversy related to this quote.)

"The prosecution on our courts for breach of promise, divorce, adultery, bigamy, seduction, rape; the newspaper reports every day of the year of scandals and outrages, of wife murderers and paramour shootings, of abortions and infanticides, are perpetual reminders of men's incapacity to cope successfully with this monster evil of society." – *Susan B. Anthony* (3)

When we look at what these early leaders of feminism said about the practice it seems that they would have more in common with today's *Feminists for Life* rather than the *National Organization of Women*.

As I think about this, that's another organization that most of you probably have never heard of due to a lack of media coverage. Who are *Feminists for life*? This organization was formed in 1972 (before *Roe V Wade*.) by Pat Goltz and Cathy Callaghan in Ohio. Goltz had been expelled by the Ohio *National Organization of Women* (though not the national organization.) for saying that abortion violated feminist principles.

These early leaders in the early '70's tried to draw attention to their cause by picketing the NOW organization convention in an attempt to draw attention to the controversy. This failed, however, due to: you guessed it, a lack of media coverage. The few media outlets that did cover it simply described it as a pro-life protest. (4)

2

Trump or Clinton?

Now, the Presidential candidates for the top office in the White House in 2016. Where do they stand on the abortion issue? Do you think you know? Read on and find out. Both candidates have made statements on the issue of abortion that have upset their constituents.

Mr. Trump has a confusing history on the abortion issue. In 1999 he claimed that he was pro-choice on the issue of abortion. Back then he was trying to appeal to the democrats while possibly considering a run for political office. Let's look at a timeline on his stand on this highly controversial issue:

April 12, 1989: Donald Trump co-sponsored a $500.00 per ticket fundraiser for NARAL (National Abortion Rights Action League.) though he does not attend the event.

October 24, 1999: Trump describes himself as very "pro-choice" to Tim Russert of *Meet the Press*. Though he says he's bothered by abortion. He answers no when asked if he would ban partial birth abortion.

October 31, 1999: "I'm totally 'pro-choice' but I hate it." *Fox News Sunday*.

December 1, 1999: "I want to see the abortion issue removed from politics." – Associated Press.

January 15, 2000: Trump changes his mind on partial birth abortion. In his book *The America We Deserve* He discusses the issue and says he changed his mind on that issue when discussing it with two doctors. (It's interesting to note that when he said he would not ban the procedure Bill Clinton was President, who vetoed a ban on the procedure. But when he said he would ban the procedure George Bush was President, who supported a ban on that procedure.)

November 18, 2010: "You will be surprised" at his position on abortion. Trump told George Stephanopoulos on ABC-TV.

February 14, 2011: "I'm Pro-life." Trump told Laura Ingraham, then later that year he repeated this stand to C-PAC the Conservative Political Action committee. And still later he told the same thing to Greta Van Susteran.

April 8, 2011: Trump explains to the Christian Broadcasting Network's *Brody File* how he came to change his views from pro-choice too pro-life.

April 19, 2011: Trump acknowledges a right to privacy but doesn't see what that has to do with abortion, on MSNBC's *Daily Run Down*.

April 29, 2011: To the New York Times he said that his position could not be negotiated and that he would appoint pro-life judges if elected.

January 24, 2015: Trump tells Bloomberg politics' Mark Halperin that he's pro-life with caveats. Listing the rape, incest and life of the mother exceptions.

June 28,2015: On Jack Tappers State of the Union Trump fumbles at first saying he's pro-choice then corrects himself.

July 22, 2015: Trump supports the 20-week abortion ban.

July 29, 2015: Trump says he would discuss the G.O.P. platform to include exceptions for rape incest and life of the mother.

August 3, 20115: Trump says he would shut down the Government to defund planned parenthood. When talking to radio host Hugh Hewitt.

August 6, 2015: Trump says he's evolved on abortion like Ronald Reagan. He said this to Fox's Megan Kelley.

August 11, 2015: Trump tells *CNN* that *Planned Parenthood* is an abortion factory but wants to look at the positive things they do.

October 18, 2015: Trump tells *Fox News* Chris Wallace that the government shouldn't be shut down over *Planned Parenthood*.

November 19, 2015: Trump tells fans at a rally in Iowa that he is for defunding *Planned Parenthood*.

December 1, 2015: Trump skirts the issue of whether or not to overturn *Roe V Wade*. This he told a rally in New Hampshire.

January 13, 2016: Trump writes that the Supreme Court's *Roe V Wade* decision led to a *culture of death*.

January 26, 2016: Trump refuses to answer if anyone should be punished for abortions at a press conference in Iowa.

February 16, 2016: Trump re-iterates his pro-life views in a statement.

February 18, 2016: Trump re-iterates that *Planned Parenthood* should be defunded on the *Brody File*.

March 30, 2016: Women should face "Some sort of Punishment." Trump tells MSNBC's Chris Matthews. Then he retracts his words in a statement later that day. He states that the doctor would be held responsible.

April 1, 2016: Trump says the laws are set. He would prefer it to be a state's rights thing but says for now they should stay that way. He said this to CBS John Dickerson. Then a spokesperson clarified later that the law shouldn't change until he's President.

April 21, 2016: Trump says he would change the Republican Party Platform to include exceptions for abortion like rape, incest and life of the mother. This he tells to NBC's Savannah Guthrie.

May 10, 2016: Trump vows to appoint justices to the supreme court who would overturn *Roe V Wade*.

May 18, 2016: Trump releases a list of names of those he'd appoint to the supreme court. He also puts a spin on his earlier statements about women being punished. He says he didn't mean they should be punished with prison but that they punish themselves. He said this to Robert Draper in an interview.

June 10, 2016: Trump says he will uphold the sanctity of human life to a joint crowd at the *Faith and Freedom Coalition* and *Concerned Women for America.*

June 30 2016: Trump says the supreme court's decision on *Whole Women's Health* wouldn't have happened if he had any say to Mike Gallagher on his radio show.

So it's easy to see where someone who votes primarily on the abortion issue, on both the pro-life and pro-choice sides, would be confused with Mr. Trump's stand on the issue. He's had to back pedal a few times and clarify his statements.

Now let's look at Hilary Clinton's stand on the issue of abortion:

January 22, 1999: Hilary re-iterated her view on "keeping abortion safe, legal and rare into the next century," remarks to NARAL. (10)

2003: Hillary referred to the unborn child as "the child, the fetus, your baby." (10)

2005: "Yes, we do have deeply held differences of opinion about the issue of abortion and I, for one, respect those who believe that there are no circumstances under which any abortion should ever be available." (10)

April, 2008: "I believe that the potential for life begins at conception." At the Compassion forum. (7)

April 2015: "Religious beliefs and structural biases have to be changed" to expand abortion. At a speech to the Women in the World Conference. (6)

January 22, 1999 ""I have met thousands and thousands of pro-choice men and women. I have never met anyone who is pro-abortion." (8)

April 3, 2016: "The Unborn Person Doesn't Have Constitutional Rights" to Chuck Todd. (10)

We can see through comments made by both Presidential candidates that they have often made confusing statements on the abortion issue which have distressed their constituents. The conservatives, for the most part, don't want abortion to be legal but don't want to discuss punishment for women who seek abortions. Most, officially anyway, do not want to seek punishment for the person who seeks the procedure.

The liberals who support Mrs. Clinton do not want to hear her call the unborn child what it is: A person. They know that if the country accepts that the child is human than that human deserves protection under the law. Which means, according to Mrs. Clinton's own statement, that she sees a certain class of person whose constitutional rights she would not support.

The liberals call the "product of conception" a "fetus" because that term sounds more scientific and dehumanizes the baby. Ironically the word fetus means "young child." (11) When does the baby form? Is it at the moment of conception? Is it alive at conception? When does the baby's heart start to beat? If the baby is alive before it is born than aborting said baby results in the baby's death.

Despite confusing statements from both camps. Trump would be better for those who are pro-life and Clinton would be better for those who are pro-choice.

3

Where did the term *War on Women* come from?

While it is a term that has existed for years. It came to prominence during the 2010 congressional elections. It refers to the passing of laws which restrict access to abortion. In the 1992 Supreme Court Decision *Planned Parenthood V Casey*, the states were given more freedom to restrict access to abortion, though they could not outlaw the procedure. (12)

The term first came into being as far back as 1989 when Andrea Dworkin wrote about a war on women in the forward to a book. Interestingly, her *war on women* had more to do with how she viewed pornography than abortion. She felt pornographers were oppressing women and using them as sex objects and waged a war on pornography.

In 1997 she published a collection of her writings called *Life and Death: Unapologetic Writings on the Continuing War Against Women*. Her argument was that the media had developed a back lash against feminist advances during the '70's. (13)

Earlier in 1991 Susan Faludi wrote a book called *Backlash: The Undeclared War Against American Women*. (14) her book came as the result of a *Newsweek* article about a study done by Harvard/Yale which talked about bleak marital prospects for single, educated career women. The statistics were apparently false so Faludi researched more articles which resulted in the book.

The book's publication date came at just the right time as the country was embroiled in the Anita Hill scandal and Gloria Steinem's own book *Revolution From Within* had been released and the two were promoted together. (14)

In 1996 Tanya Melich wrote a memoir entitled *The Republican War Against Women: An Insider's Report from Behind the Lines.* Describes how the pro-life movement and opposition to the equal rights amendment were incorporated into Republicans way of thinking and how it was divergent from feminist causes. (15)

In 2004 the feminist press published Laura Flanders collection of articles *The W Effect: Bush's War On Women.* And in 2006 Zed books published Laura Flanders critique of the Bush Presidency called *George W. Bush and the War on Women: Turning Back the Clock on Progress.* (16), (17)

All of these publications led Debbie Wasserman Schultz, then chairman of the Democratic party, who has since been forced to resign in disgrace, to begin using the term *war on women.* Aggressive feminists have documented legislation that Republicans have enacted to restrict access to abortion.

 Proponents of this legislation claim that these laws will protect women from unhealthy facilities and practices. Opponents of these laws claim that they are unfairly limiting the free exercise of "choice" and undermining the Supreme Court decision that originally tore down all restrictions imposed by the states on abortion in 1973: *Roe V Wade.*

According to Democratic strategist Zerlina Maxwell, there have been 135 pieces of legislation enacted that affect "reproductive rights" and she declared that the Republican war on women is no fiction. (18)

But what are the laws that she is talking about? Are they really restrictive? Are they pro-woman or anti-woman? Can a person be pro-life and pro-woman? A lot of women claim to be pro-life in this country. What are those women's views on "reproductive health?" Does this mean that there are women involved in fighting against women's rights?

We've already seen that early feminists thought that abortion was deplorable. There is also a movement called "Feminists for Life" but there are other conservative women's organizations such as "Concerned Women for America" who oppose "reproductive rights." We'll take a look at what those groups have to say. But now, let's look at the casualties in the real war on women.

4

Casualties?

There are casualties in this war? Some may ask, and the answer is yes. In fact, there are many casualties in the war on women, but I'm not talking about the ones you may think I'm talking about. There are women who have been seriously injured, maimed and killed by so-called "reproductive rights." You won't hear about these victims in the mainstream media because the news media looks the other way and does not report on said victims because doing so might throw a bad light on their precious Planned Parenthood.

The liberal considers an abortion gone wrong, resulting in the live birth of the baby that the abortionist was trying to kill, a "dreaded complication." Let's stop and consider this for just a moment. A baby being born alive is something that the pro-choice individual considers to be dreaded. The majority of people, at least the ones I know, consider a baby's birth to be a beautiful thing.

Doctor Willard Cates, former head of the CDC's Abortion Surveillance group, was quoted in the Philadelphia Inquirer of August 2, 1981 as saying, "(Live births) are little known because organized medicine, from fear of public clamor and legal action, treats them more as an embarrassment to be hushed up than a problem to be solved. It's like turning yourself in to the IRS for an audit. ... The tendency is not to report because there are only negative incentives." Cates estimates that 400 to 500 abortion live births occur every year in the U.S (19)

400 to 500 live births per year. What happens to a baby born alive in an abortion clinic? What happens to the person that attacks said baby and tries to take their lives? Who are these individuals and what do they have to say about the procedure that attempted to destroy their lives? Let's discuss some of these cases. Remember,

according to Hilary Clinton these people "Had no constitutional rights." First let's look at the victims.

An Abortion Survivor's Story

In September of 1975, a woman discovered that she was pregnant. Things were very difficult for her, as she was raising two sons, six and 15 years old. Their father had walked out on them and refused to help care for the boys financially, or in any other way. The only alternative for this woman, it seemed, was to abort this unexpected baby. After all, she could barely afford to feed the children she already had.

Between the months of September 1975 and January 1976, this woman had three therapeutic abortions in an attempt to rid herself of the unborn baby. These abortions, also known as a "salting out procedure" are performed by injecting a very large syringe into the woman's abdomen, removing a certain amount of amniotic fluid out of the womb, and then injecting three times the amount of saline back in, thus "burning" the baby out. For reasons only God knows, these abortions did not take and on April 21, 1976, two months premature, her baby was born. The child was perfect and healthy, weighing four pounds, five ounces.

Unfortunately, on March 16, 1977, the mother passed away, less than a year after her baby girl was born. After the woman's death, the infant's father and paternal grandmother took custody of the baby and her two brothers. As this baby girl grew up, her father told her about the three abortions she had undergone in her mother's womb but this little girl never believed him, as she assumed that if a baby is aborted, he or she could not possibly survive.

The truth only came to this girl when she was eighteen years old, married, and approximately five months pregnant with her first child. This girl needed and soon obtained her mother's medical records from the hospital that had treated her. Imagine her utter shock as she read about how her mother tried to terminate her unborn child three times. As the young girl read the medical documents, the new life inside of her was stirring and kicking as if to say "Mommy please don't get any ideas."

Today this young woman is 25 years old and is raising a family of her own. She is healthy and normal in every way, with no physical deformities of any kind.

I am the child that I have been writing about. My mother had no right to try and abort me, no matter what the circumstances were, no matter how inconvenient her pregnancy was. And if she was here with us today, I'm sure she would agree. Life is too precious to simply throw away. Now I can speak out against abortion from the baby's perspective. Any baby would choose life.

- Amy (20)

That is one testimony from a young lady named "Amy" no other information is given on Amy, apparently she wishes to remain anonymous. But there are many others who do not remain anonymous. They want their stories known and are spokespeople for the unborn children who are helpless and cannot speak for themselves.

The news media completely ignores their stories which makes it difficult for them to make their cases known to the majority of Americans. They continue to speak at pro-life meetings and political gatherings around the country in hopes that there will be a few people among the crowd that haven't heard their stories and will respond.

How can these people not have rights in a free country? Mrs. Clinton and her followers may not feel that these people should have constitutional rights but they do have rights, inalienable human rights, which we, as a nation, have been violating since 1973. (21)

I'm going to introduce you to several of these people now and let you decide for yourself whether they should have rights under the constitution of the United States of America to coincide with their inalienable human rights, which no one can deny, not even Hilary Clinton.

Abortion survivor Gianna Jessen.

Gianna Jessen

The next survivor I'd like to talk about in the war on women is Gianna Jessen. Her story can be found on line. (21) I had the privilege of interviewing Gianna on my radio show in 1995. She was very young at the time. A bright and vivacious girl who is undaunted in her support for the rights of the un-born.

Jessica Shaver is the author who brought Gianna's story to life in a beautifully written novel that is available on line.

Who is Gianna Jessen? When did this abortion happen? Who aborted Gianna?

The answers are in this book and it is a strong testimony to the cold indifference of the human race toward someone who has survived a procedure that was deemed legal in all 50 States in 1973.

A compelling read. I read it the week before I interviewed her in 1995.

She began life in 1977 as her mother, Tina, decided to have an abortion at the age of 17. She was only two months away from being born. The man who aborted Gianna was Dr. Edward Allred. In the review section of her amazon book page (22) Jessica Shaver reports that Dr. Allred stated that in those days they didn't have the technology to be sure how far along a pregnancy was so he "guestimated." He wound up not using enough of the saline solution it would have taken to kill her. Now I want you all to let this sink in for a minute. THIS DOCTOR GUESTIMATED ON

HOW MUCH SALINE SOLUTION TO USE. This is "safe and legal" abortion? How is this safe for Gianna? Can any doctor just guestiamate on what to do before performing a medical procedure? Is an anesthesiologist allowed to just guess before administering medication? (see Marla Cardamone.) Why are abortion industry "professionals" not subject to the same standards as other medical industry professionals?

The recent Supreme Court case, *Whole Woman's Health v. Hellerstedt* struck down a Texas law that would have required abortion providers to adhere to the same standards as other medical providers. Planned Parenthood is allowed to police themselves. No one can tell them what to do (unlike the rest of the medical field.) This is why we get monsters like Abu Hyatt, Kermit Gosnell, and Edward Allred. We will discuss them and more in a later chapter.

Look at where we've come since 1973. Back then you couldn't describe the baby as what it is; a human being. They were just "globs of tissue," "products of conception," "fetal matter." These terms and others are still used today. And they never call the child a "baby," they always use the word "fetus" It sounds more scientific and less human. Even though the word means "young child."

We also couldn't casually talk about how much saline solution was used to try and kill the fetus. That would have been taboo. This is progress? This is "Reproductive Health Care?" This was done in the name of "choice?" What kind of Orwellian Newspeak are today's spin doctors using to justify destroying human life?

For the record this isn't health care at all. Aborting a healthy child from its healthy mother's womb is not healthy for either. In my opinion this kind of abomination has to be stopped.

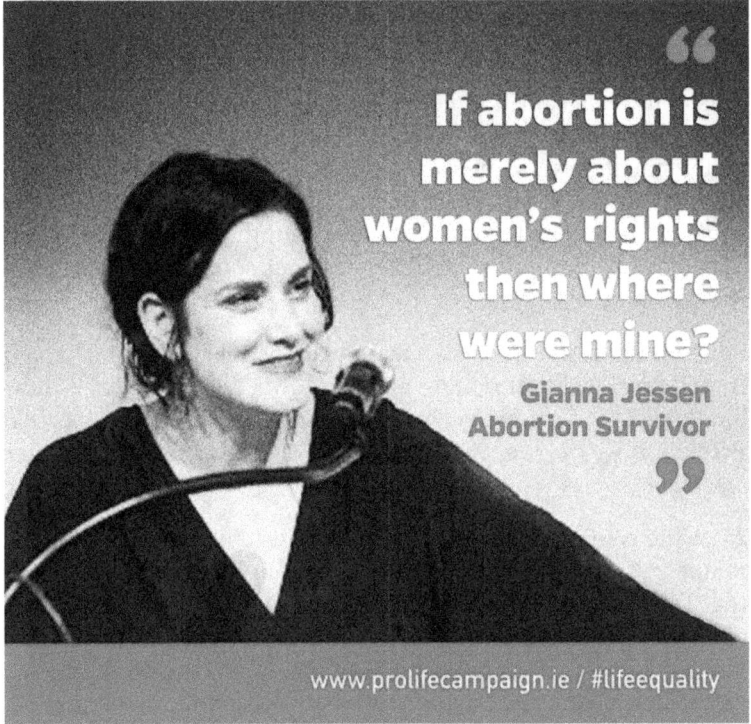

If abortion is merely about women's rights then where were mine?

Gianna Jessen
Abortion Survivor

www.prolifecampaign.ie / #lifeequality

Gianna Jessen is a born again Christian and makes no apologies for her Christian faith. In fact, as a result of the saline solution used in the abortion, she has cerebral palsy and spina bifida. She does not look on these conditions as handicaps. She describes her cerebral palsy as a "gift." She says this condition allowed her to "depend on Jesus for everything."

Doctors and scientists were wrong about Gianna. They predicted that she wouldn't be able to even lift her head let alone walk. But Gianna being the tough as nails individual she is defied the odds. Not only is she not a drooling vegetable, but she has run marathons. I guess the science wasn't "settled."

Gianna travels the world to share her incredible story. In Italy she was featured on one of their most popular afternoon talk shows and the Pope shared her story in the Vatican newspaper. She was also profiled in the Italian edition of Vanity Fair. In America she's been on CBN and shows like Maury Povich. She's also featured in blogs on the internet around the world like China and Australia.

You can find her amazing stories on YouTube in speeches that she's given at Yale and the aforementioned Australia.

President Bush said "I'm not going to let you down" when he met her in 2002. Indeed, she's addressed congress twice and watched as President Bush signed the *Infants born alive act*. Sadly, the current President (Obama) does not have her back. His party supports abortion throughout all 9 months of Pregnancy and opposes the *Infants born Alive act*. As it somehow undermines *Roe V Wade*.

Can you imagine what a slap in the face that is to Gianna? To go from a President that wouldn't let her down, indeed, the most pro-life President that we've ever had, to the most pro-abortion President we've ever had who won't even acknowledge her existence.

After the signing, the president (Bush) visited with her for just a moment. "What he said will remain with me always. The reason is that I've never heard these words from a father. He looked at me and said 'You are so sweet.' He repeated, 'You are so sweet, and I'm not going to let you down." He then, kissed me on the cheek, hugged me again, and went on his way." – Gianna Jessen (21)

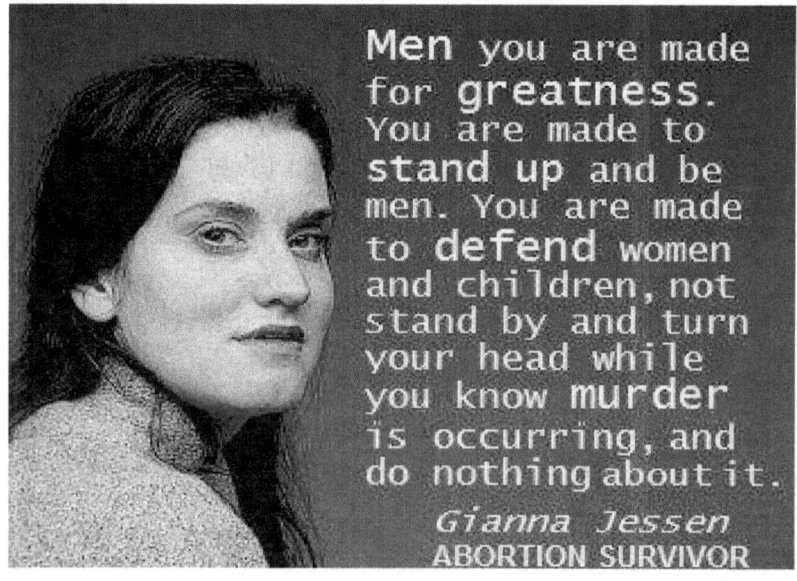

Men you are made for greatness. You are made to stand up and be men. You are made to defend women and children, not stand by and turn your head while you know murder is occurring, and do nothing about it.
Gianna Jessen
ABORTION SURVIVOR

Here is Gianna's testimony:

Testimony of abortion survivor Gianna Jessen before the Constitution Subcommittee of the house of Judiciary Committee in April 22, 1996

My name is Gianna Jessen. I am 19 years of age and I am originally from California, but now reside in Franklin, Tennessee. I am adopted and I have cerebral palsy. My biological mother was 17 years old, and seven and one-half months pregnant when she made the decision to have a Saline Abortion. I am the person she Aborted! I lived instead of died!

Fortunately, the abortionist was not in the clinic when I arrived Alive, instead of Dead! At 6:00 a.m. on the morning of April 6, 1977. I was early. My death was not expected to be seen until about 9:00 a.m.; when he would probably be arriving for his office hours. I am sure that I would not be here today if the abortionist would have been in the clinic as his job is to Take Life, not Sustain it! Some have said I am a "botched abortion; a result of a job not well done. I remained in the hospital for almost three months. There was not much hope for me in the beginning. I weighed only two pounds. Today, babies smaller than I have survived.

A doctor once said that I had a great will to live and fought for my life. I eventually was able to leave the hospital and be placed in foster care. I was diagnosed with cerebral palsy as a result of the abortion.

My foster mother was told that it was doubtful that I would ever crawl or walk. I could no sit up independently. Through the prayers and dedication of my foster mother, and later many other people, I eventually learned to sit up, crawl, and then started to stand. I walked with leg braces and a walker shortly before I turned to the age of four; and I was legally adopted by my foster mother's daughter, Diana De Paul a few months after I began to walk. The Department of Social Services would not release me any earlier for adoption. (26)

You can find Gianna's testimony on YouTube if you'd like to watch it for yourself.

Ana Rosa Rodriquez

Warning: graphic description: Here is a truly tragic case and is good testimony to the idea that ultrasound should be necessary before aborting a child. You see Ana Rosa Rodriguez was born without her right arm. What happened to her arm? It was torn off before she was born by abortionist Abu Hyatt in New York. Unlike Gianna she keeps a low profile about what happened to her also the abortionist that tried to kill her did time in jail, while Gianna's abortionist did not.

Everyone would agree that what happened to Ana Rosa should never happen.

Ana Rosa Rodriguez, 18 months old.

Ana's right arm was severed by an abortionist during an abortion attempt when her mother was 7½ months pregnant...

Photo © New York Post 1991

Nat Hentoff reported for the *Washington Post*: "Ana Rosa Rodriguez was born in 1991 without a right arm. Actually, she was not supposed to have been born. Her mother, 19-year-old Rosa Rodriguez, a Dominican immigrant, 7 1/2 months pregnant, had gone to Dr. Abu Hayat on New York's Lower East Side for an abortion. It was botched; Ana Rosa was born the day after. But in the course of the doctor's attempts to dismember her the day before, Ana Rosa's right arm had been torn off."

The 19-year-old Rosa Rodriguez had gone to Dr. Hyatt seeking an abortion, apparently not knowing how far along her pregnancy was. When Dr. Hyatt removed her right arm he was startled. You see, he did not verify Ana Rosa's gestational age before attempting the procedure. When he realized what he had done, he went into the waiting room and demanded more money from the gentleman that Rosa came in with. When he told Hyatt that he didn't have any more money the good doctor woke Rosa up and sent the couple home.

That's right the good doctor Hyatt sent her home. Rosa and her companion weren't sent to the hospital, oh no. This wonderful abortion humanitarian *sent a woman home with a mutilated child still in her womb*! All in the name of *reproductive health care*. This was healthy? This was choice? Any number of things could have gone wrong, not just with Ana but her mother too.

Fortunately, Rosa had enough presence of mind to sue. Unlike Gianna's mother, who had only been 17, Rosa was 19. A little older and a little wiser. Gianna's mother didn't have enough presence of mind to sue the man who tried to kill Gianna.

From Nat Hentoff: "In February of this year, a jury in New York State Supreme Court convicted Dr. Hayat on a number of counts. One was performing an illegal abortion in the third trimester of pregnancy. While 11 states permit abortions during the final three months, New York prohibits it after 24 weeks."

If the so-called Freedom of Choice act were to pass than doctors like Hyatt might get off scott free because it leaves the age of viability up to the practicing Physician. As Hentoff himself noted in his article a sonogram would have shown Ana Rosa to be a healthy viable baby, within a month of being born. And yet, according to today's liberal politician it's somehow punishing women to allow them to see a sonogram of their unborn baby. As we'll see in a later chapter, Ana wasn't Hyatt's only victim. (23)

Ocala Star Banner - Feb 25, 1993 Browse this newspaper. Browse all newspapers.

Mother plans to tell daughter of botched abortion attempt

By Samuel Maull
Associated Press Writer

NEW YORK — A woman whose daughter was mutilated in a botched abortion says she'll be straightforward when the girl asks why she's missing an arm.

"I will tell her the truth," Rosa Rodriguez said. Ana Rosa Rodriguez, 16 months, lost her arm when Dr. Abu Hayat sliced it off during an attempted abortion while her mother was almost eight months pregnant.

Hayat, 63, was convicted Monday on assault and illegal abortion charges for trying to terminate Rodriguez's pregnancy when it had progressed beyond 24 weeks and for maiming Ana Rosa.

Rodriguez, 22, told reporters in her lawyer's office Tuesday that she was happy Hayat was convicted. She said she knew he would be, and she hopes for a long prison term when he is sentenced March 15.

Hayat faces five to 15 years in prison on each of three first-degree assault counts, the most serious charges on which he was convicted. The maximum sentence for illegal abortion is 16 months to four years.

Rodriguez, an unemployed waitress, testified at Hayat's trial that she found his name in a Spanish-language newspaper. Already a single mother of a little girl, she went to Hayat on Oct. 25, 1991, not knowing how long she had been pregnant.

A Hayat assistant, Rabia Basri, 24, testified that on the second day of what was expected to be a two-day procedure, she saw Hayat tossing flesh into a garbage pail.

Assistant District Attorney Margaret Finerty suggested in her summation that this discarded flesh was Ana Rosa's arm.

Hayat sent Rodriguez home, expecting her to return a third day. But pain overwhelmed her and she went to Jamaica Hospital where Ana Rosa was born with her right arm missing.

Jeffrey Lichtman, Rodriguez's lawyer, said Ana Rosa "romps and plays and is a very happy, rambunctious, gregarious child" who does not yet seem to be aware of her disability.

How to help

Contributions to the Ana Rosa Rodriguez Fund may be sent to Trofman & Glaser, 575 Lexington Ave., New York, N.Y., 10022.

Sixteen-month old Ana Rosa Rodriguez appeared with her mother at a news conference.

21

Sarah Smith

In another case that is a strong argument for ultrasound, or sonogram laws, which the current administration views as unnecessary, Sarah Smith survived an abortion attempt in 1970, three years before *Roe V Wade,* in a state that had already legalized abortion, California.

In this story Sarah's mother sought out an abortion and the abortionist, another great humanitarian that made sure he knew what he was doing (sarcasm,) did not realize that her mother was carrying twins. After the abortion, the doctor informed her that she was still pregnant and that she had been carrying twins. Her mother was devastated when she heard this and somehow the reality of what was done sunk in and she refused another abortion.

Her son, Andrew was killed but her daughter Sarah, survived. This casualty in the war on women suffered bilateral, congenital dislocated hips and other handicaps as a result of being attacked before she was born. Sarah had tiny casts applied to her legs which had to be replaced once a week and has to wear a body cast to this day. I'm going to reprint a speech that Sarah made while in Rome:

On April 24, 1996, Sarah Smith gave the following speech at an international pro-life conference in Rome. The conference was called, **"A Congress for Life."** It was organized to celebrate the first anniversary of Pope John Paul II's encyclical letter **Evangelium Vitae - The Gospel of Life**. The conference was held at the Legionaries of Christ seminary in Rome and was attended by approximately 500 men and women including; pro-life leaders, political leaders, media representatives, priests and seminarians. Following is the speech given by Sarah Smith:

"My name is Sarah Smith and I wish to thank you all, your eminencies, and all of the wonderful Legionaries of Christ for allowing us to be with you today. I did not know of the abortion until I was 12 years old. I grew up feeling that I was the same as my friends, except for having numerous surgeries and physical complications. The only difference I felt was an incredible loneliness and a knowledge that something was missing. I never felt whole. I battled with severe depression and found myself dying of anorexia nervosa at age 12, when my mother knew it was time to tell me the truth.

She sat next to me and took my hand and looked me in the eyes and said, "Sarah, you are a twin. I aborted your twin brother and tried to abort you. Please know I did not know what I was doing and I pray someday you are able to forgive me. I love you and need you to know that you are a welcome part of our family."

At that moment I knew what I had been missing all my life and that I was called to something much greater than I had knowledge of. Immediately I felt the overwhelming pain of the knowledge that I should be dead. As I stand before you today I am painfully aware that this is only possible because my twin brother took a scalpel for me, and I stand in his place and memory, giving him honor and a face.

We have become bombarded with statistics in our fight for life. Thirty-two million babies are killed in the United States alone. Yet everyone had a face, a life, a creator who loved them and created them in His image. As you look at me today, you realize that I am no different than you, yet I stand before you today a representative of the dead -- a representative of the innocent lives who today may lose their lives. Who will speak for them?

The words of Christ are clear - "What you have done to the least of these you have done unto me." You and I are called and commissioned to care for these little ones just as we would care for Jesus Himself. To walk away and say this is not my problem is to walk away from Jesus Himself.

Many people upon finding out about the abortion ask me how did I feel, or to what can I compare this to. The only thing I can compare my life to is that of an innocent Jew being made to walk down the streets of Germany naked in front of many people and into a room he knows he will never come out of. In my case, unfortunately, the people leading me into that room are my mother and father. Yet the people looking on at the sidelines are people like you. And I ask you today, will you speak up or will you silently look away as another person who needs your help is led to their death?

I have forgiven my parents long ago as I remember the words Jesus spoke as he hung bleeding and bruised from the cross, "Forgive them Father for they know not what they do." His words pertain to the sins of abortion. Most men and women who involve themselves with abortion don't know what they're doing, as were my parents.

Many women who demand the right to an abortion say, "It's my body, it's my choice." Let me make one thing very clear to you today - my mother's choice was my death sentence. It is not only a woman's body we are discussing in an abortion. It is the entire flesh and blood of someone just like me.

Then we have the issue of medical personnel stating it is just tissue. For anyone who has ever studied biology, you know better. Before any woman even knows she is pregnant her child already has a beating heart at 20 days. Show me one piece of tissue or cancer you believe must be cut out with a beating heart. Show me a liver or kidney that has its own blood type. That child is perfect from its first day. All it needs is time, oxygen and nutrition.

Another startling fact is that in medical journals it states the fetus is capable of feeling pain at 8 weeks of gestation. In America, the vast majority of abortions are performed between 10 to 12 weeks, well after the child can feel the entire procedure. So don't tell me abortion is a simple procedure that expels a piece of tissue and doesn't hurt anybody. I was there. I was less than an inch away from my innocent twin brother when his body was ripped apart, and he felt the entire thing. We were 14 to 16 weeks along in the second trimester. That was how my life was meant to end.

Yet I was spared to stand before you today and tell you on behalf of those who have no voice that if you remain silent, in my country alone a person just like you and me will die every 20 seconds of every day. We have been commissioned by Jesus to speak up for those who cannot speak for themselves and we have also been commissioned by the Holy Father, who I had the privilege of meeting a few hours ago.

As I told him my story he looked at me so intensely as if to say, "Speak the message! Proclaim the Truth!" And then he kissed me and gave me a blessing to go and speak about life. And that is what he says to all of you as he blesses and kisses us with his Encyclical. Preach the gospel - the good news of life. What is the greatest gift of all? When Jesus outstretched His arms and said, "This is my body given up for you". Imagine if Jesus had been selfish with His body and not given so freely of His life to you and me. Where would we be today? We would be nothing. The gift of a mother's body for 9 months of her life is one of the most beautiful gifts of all time. We must fight to protect it.

As I stand here alone knowing I have my brother as a precious guardian angel who is with me always, I know my life is a gift. And today I wish to give it back to you, the people and to the church, as a symbol of the consuming power of God's redemption and of His life and truth. You and I as a church represent life, and together we will extend that life into a hurting and dying world. We will give them the truth of life and we shall never be silent.

I love you and God bless you."

After surviving her mother's abortion in 1970, Sarah Smith has become one of the most powerful pro-life voices in the battle against abortion. Sarah's stirring testimony touches hearts, changes minds and saves lives. Sarah wants to help you make a difference in your community. Please order Sarah's video today and share it with people at churches, schools, rallies and conferences in your community.

This powerful 10-minute documentary was produced by the 700 Club -- and it's one you'll never forget. You'll see Sarah as a baby crawling in a body-cast, then as a teenager and later as a dynamic public speaker who travels the world exposing the pain and suffering caused by abortion. When you see Sarah, you're seeing the face of a beautiful woman who would not be alive today if the abortionist had completed his "job." (24)

Call Heritage House toll-free at 1-800-858-3040 and mention Pro-Life America's web site.

Ximena Renaerts

The war is not only being waged in the U.S. it is being waged in neighboring Canada as well. Indeed, it is being waged worldwide. But I want to focus on one survivor in Canada. In a flagrant violation of human rights. On December 16, 1985 Ximena came into this world at Vancouver General Hospital and was placed in a room where dead (how did they die?) fetuses were stored. She was still gasping and breathing.

A nurse checked the room later and found that she was still alive. By the time she had received proper medical care, she had suffered major heat loss which led too permanent, excessive brain damage. The adoptive family sued VGH for $10 million. At first they didn't seem to have a case because the Attorney General was pro-abortion but Canadian Right to Life activists brought attention to the case and it was discovered that this had happened before. The Hospital settled with the family out of court.

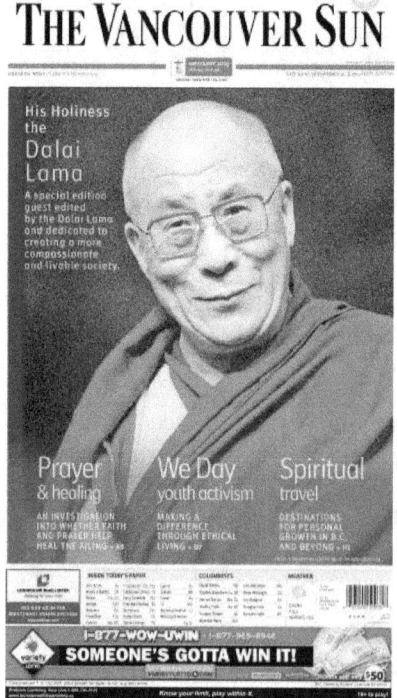

A Vancouver Sun article dated May 30, 1986 noted that nurse Kathryn Larouche described how three infants had died after being born alive. Larouche described how they were just supposed to leave it alone. That they would eventually die. She eventually resigned after not being able to deal with the inhuman conditions found there. Five others left with her. The Hospital claims that no other viable babies died. (26)

How many other babies were aborted and came into this world alive at this hospital and were left to die? When are we going to wake up and stop these atrocities?

Heidi Huffman

Just a year after Gianna Jessen was aborted, 17-year-old Tina Huffman, who came from a broken, dysfunctional home, found herself pregnant with her boyfriend's baby. The entire family, including her boyfriend's parents, were adamant that she had to have an abortion. She was not offered any other option (only one "choice?") So, the naive teenager, thinking that there were no other options, went into an abortion clinic.

Tina signed a waiver, paid $150.00 in cash, then took a valium. She laid down next to a suction machine. When the suction started she said that "...her body started to vibrate. I felt my insides being pulled out, all of them." When she exclaimed to the nurse that she was dying the nurse coldly told her to empty her bladder.

When the "procedure" was done the nurse reacted in surprise and said: "You're not bleeding." Tina was then discharged with birth control pills and anti-biotics.

Tina was sick for about two months when she was told that her abortion failed. It was suggested to her that she should get a lawyer. She couldn't understand how the procedure could have failed and wondered what to do. She didn't want to go through the painful abortion again and thought about the unborn child growing inside of her. What was the baby's destiny?

In the months to follow, Tina's fear increased when three amniocenteses produced blood instead of amniotic fluid. Tina finally decided to see an attorney. She gathered all the paper work that she had regarding the abortion and her lawyer phoned the clinic where she had undergone the operation.

After an intense phone call the clinic conveniently "lost" Tina's file and her attorney informed her that he couldn't do anything else for her. There wasn't any evidence that she had been at the clinic and, apparently, the attorney didn't want to try and prove she was there.

At 28 weeks' gestation her doctor performed an examination on her and, after an emergency C-Section a beautiful baby girl came into this world named Heidi Huffman.

Tina and Heidi travel the country speaking out on pro-life issues and do sidewalk counseling at abortion clinics, trying to convince women that there is a better way than aborting the child they carry in their womb.

Abortion survivor Heidi Huffman

"I was a survivor of Abortion: I can remain silent no more."

I present Audrey's testimony in her own words: "One day when I was in third grade, my mom and dad asked me to sit down for a talk. They began by saying that since I was very little, my parents always found me sleeping curled tightly in the fetal position, buried in the covers and always to one side of the bed. I had a recurring nightmare of being trapped in a room with a window blocked by a knife, and they said they often found me talking to my "other self." My mom said she thought these were signs telling her to confess something she had done and hoped I would forgive her.

She told me how, at 39, with her 5 children grown, (the youngest was 19 years old and two were in college), she had found herself pregnant. She had been pressured especially by a particular friend to abort because she was too old and it would be "ridiculous" at her age, to have a baby. This was 1952, and her friend told her a self-abortion method. She delayed her abortion attempt until the end of June, her eldest son Elliott's, birthday. She was about 3 months pregnant.

She started to cry and told me never to believe them when they tell you it is not a baby, but just a blob of tissue. Tracing a tiny outline in the palm of her hand, she said "he was this big and a fully formed baby." She could hardly continue. "He was a perfect little baby boy." She cried to heaven on that cold bathroom floor and asked God to forgive her and promised Him if she were ever to become pregnant again, she would NEVER abort a baby. She flushed her little son down the toilet and said she lay on the cold floor crying until she was numb.

No one knew, except her and her so called "friend." Later, she still felt pregnant. The doctor said that I was probably a tumor or an ulcer. And the first part of September, I kicked her! The doctor was amazed that I had been a hiding twin and survived the abortion attempt. She told no one of her pregnancy except my dad, and later, my youngest brother, 19-year-old Fred, who I kicked.

I was due January 21, 1953, however, I was induced one month early on December 19, 1952, and after 3 days of labor, I was born at the

Hour of Mercy, 3:30 P.M., Sunday, December 21, 1952. She asked me to forgive her. I asked if she loved me NOW because she did not know me then. She sobbed and sobbed and said, "Yes. I love you with my very life." I said, "Ok," and walking back down the hall to my room I could still hear her heartbreaking sobs. When my dad hurried and caught my arm, he whispered, "I did not do it." And pointing to Mom, he said, "She did!" And I believe the Holy Spirit said this to him through me: "But your love was supposed to make her feel safe to have me." Those words hit his heart and stopped him from coming any further. (Note: I never slept curled up or had nightmares after this day.)

Years came and went. My mom's "illness" without a name was cyclical and caused her to take to her bed from the end of June to the beginning of September. Sometimes she flew into rages, or walked the floors night after night, or went on buying binges. She suffered from paranoia, and gobbled down her doctor's pills. This led to stays in mental hospitals, filled with psychotropic drugs and painful electroshock therapy. Part of the therapy was to tell her it was shame abortion was not legal then, because she could have gone to college, had a career...and not wasted her talents. I remember when I looked deeply into her drugged eyes and told her one summer day, "I know my mom is in there somewhere and some day when I grow up, I am going to find out what this illness is!" We all suffered. Around me I saw other moms with similar problems and obsessions. Now we were living in the days of Roe v. Wade. Imagine the scope of my mom's pain from just one abortion attempt, and now women have multiple abortions! Three months before my mom died, I asked her why all the breakdowns June through September every year. Why? she broke down in tears and said it was on Elliott's birthday (the end of June) that she aborted my brother and when Elliott had died tragically at age 27, she felt she had caused the death of her first born son when she aborted her last son. By September she remembered the day I kicked her and how happy she was, and that would bring her out of her moods. She could not trust herself and hated herself for aborting her baby! How could God forgive her? It was a form of self-punishment for a crime she felt she could not be forgiven. I told her that is why Jesus died and that God forgave her when she found out that she was still pregnant with me. He trusted her to give me life. She never saw this until the day I told her. Three months later she died, but at peace, and forgiven.

Then and now, silence from the pulpit, the medical and psychiatric communities keep this killing cycle going. Now we have a name for the "illness." It is post-abortion syndrome. But physicians and women's (so called "rights groups") do not even recognize it. How many suffer in silence, looking for help. Yet, we live in an age where Project Rachel groups, St. Raphael Ministries retreats, and prolife organizations are breaking through the silence barrier and helping all the victims of abortion to find healing through the cross of Jesus and the life giving sacraments, especially Reconciliation.

I can remain silent no more. I was a survivor of abortion. Life is never a mistake; life is always a blessing from God. Every single person has a divine mission that only they can fulfill.

The Bible says, "...and a child shall lead them." It is the worst of times because of great sin, but it is the best of times because of an abundance of God's grace. Love is a decision. Let us decide to be silent no more."

Audrey (29)

That is a look at a few of the babies that survived an attack on their lives. Some of them have severe defects as a result of the attack, others have minimal defects. They all have been injured either physically, emotionally or both.

In the next chapter I want to talk about some of the mothers that have been injured or killed in this attack on women in this country. It is real, it is sobering and it is a tragic shame.

5

Hidden Statistics

Woman are told all the time that the abortion procedure is harmless. There is no child, they say. It's only a "globe of tissue," "product of conception," "a fetus." They never call the child what it is; a baby that has just formed in its mother's womb. As we've seen in the last chapter all of this is mis-information. These are very much human beings who deserve their own right to life. As Hilary Clinton has noted these persons do not have constitutional rights. However, they should because they do have inalienable human rights that have been violated. When the constitution fails to protect a certain class of person how long will it be before the constitution fails to protect the rest of us?

Pro-choice activists use the case of Rosie Jimenez who died from an illegal abortion in 1977 to argue for "safe and legal" abortions. Abortion was legalized in all 50 states in 1973 but the Hyde amendment made it illegal for federal funding of abortion. This was Ms. Jimenez third abortion and she couldn't get this one for free. Therefore, she sought an illegal one at a low price.

This abortion resulted in an incomplete procedure and Jimenez experienced severe cramping and went to the hospital. She lied about the abortion but medical professionals realized the truth after examining her. They performed emergency surgery on her and gave her antibiotics but it was all to no avail. Rosie passed away as a result of abortion complications.

The media wasted no time in spreading the word that Rosie Jimenez could not get a free abortion and died as a result. The truth of the matter is that Jimenez could have paid the right price for her abortion, but she "chose" to get an illegal abortion at a cheaper price. That lower price cost her her life as well as the life of the child in her womb. (29)

32

The full story of Rosie's death was chronicled in an investigative publication by Ellen Frankfurt called *Rosie: The Investigation of a Wrongful Death*. (30)

But isn't it true that there was an increase in death from illegal abortions following the Hyde amendment? Yes, there was. But there was also an increase in deaths from legally obtained abortions as well: "There was indeed a small spike in reported illegal abortion deaths after the Hyde Amendment (from 2 in 1976 to 4 in 1977 to 7 in 1978). But there was likewise a spike in reported *legal* abortion deaths as well -- a far larger spike, from 11 in 1976 to 17 in 1977." (29)

This was an illegal death in 1977. But what about before 1973? Before Roe V Wade? Were there illegal deaths from obtaining abortion in the era before Roe? Of course there were! Most abortions before the Penicillin era, which is before 1930 (31) were highly dangerous to the mother. It probably wouldn't have mattered much at that time whether the procedure was legal or not, their probably would have been the same amount of deaths.

But what about after 1930? The number of women's lives that ended because of illegal abortion steadily declined. In 1972 (the year before abortion was federally legalized), a total of 24 women died from causes known to be associated with legal abortions, and 39 died as a result of known illegal abortions. (32)

In 1964 28-year-old Gerri Santoro died from an illegally obtained abortion. She is another symbol for the pro-choice movement. The year before she left her husband, Sam Santoro due to domestic violence. They had married after meeting each other at a bus stop.

After returning to her childhood home of Mansfield Gerri developed a relationship with Clyde Dixon and she became pregnant. When she learned that Sam was going to come visit his daughters Santoro panicked. She, while 6 ½ months pregnant, was in fear for her life and decided to have an abortion. She and Dixon checked into a motel room in Norwich CT. Dixon himself performed the abortion using a text book and medical instruments obtained from a co-worker at the school. When Santoro began to hemorrhage Dixon panicked and fled. He did not try to find medical help and left his girlfriend to die in the motel. Gerri was discovered by a maid the next morning. Dixon was convicted of manslaughter and conspiracy to commit abortion.

I mention Gerri's story here because the pro-choice activists have used her story and the photograph of her nude body that police took at the motel room as a poster child for the pro-choice cause. The media sensationalized her death which further aided their argument and cause until, 9 years later, the U.S. Supreme Court struck down all state laws regarding the illegality of abortion and unleashed a fight that goes on to this day between pro-life and pro-choice activists. (33)

FIGURE 2. Maternal mortality rate,* by year — United States, 1900–1997

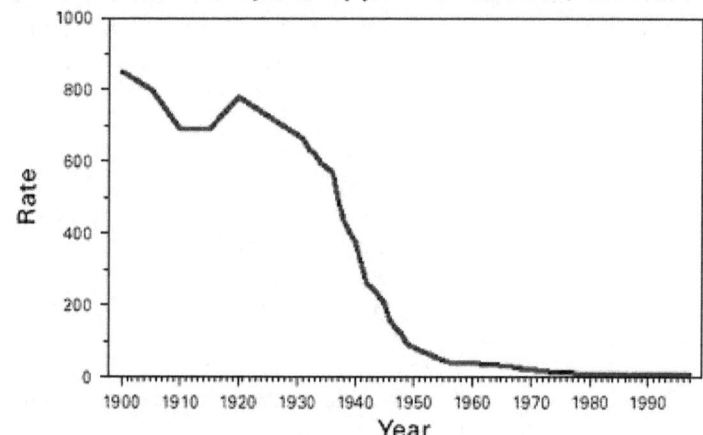

*Per 100,000 live births.

As you can see by this chart, abortion related deaths had dropped significantly before the Roe V Wade decision. After 1930 and the introduction of penicillin the fatalities took a steep plunge. (35)

We've mentioned two who have died from illegally induced abortions. But what about women who've died from legally induced abortions? Now that abortion is safe and legal no one is dying from abortion related complications anymore right? You'd be led to think that considering how little you've heard about women who have died from legally induced abortion in the mainstream news media. As I was working on this chapter I came across this article from Dr.

Alveda King, who is the niece of civil rights leader Martin Luther King Jr.:

Timed to coincide with the 53rd anniversary of the Rev. Dr. Martin Luther King's "I Have a Dream Speech," Priests for Life's African-American Outreach is launching a new web page, logo, mascot and name – Civil Rights for the Unborn.

As director of Priests for Life African American Outreach, we interrupt this announcement of unveiling our new "Civil Rights for the Unborn" website at **www.civilrightsfortheunborn.com** to report more death from yet another abortion.

Mounting grief over yet more deaths after having an abortion — this time of Michigan mother Cree Erwin and baby — overshadows our news. Black leaders and pro-life leaders at large are outraged and grieved that yet another young beautiful black woman and her baby have recently succumbed to painful deaths following an abortion.

In the aftermath of Erwin's abortion death, one of many in America, Pastor Clennard Childress, co-founder of L.E.A.R.N. says: "Black Life Matters has [recently] teamed up with the most destructive racist machine in American history; its founder, Margaret Sanger was the most devout racist of her time!"

"The leading killer of innocent unarmed African-Americans in the womb — whose hands were up, but given no choice or chance at the American dream their fellow African American, Dr. Martin Luther King preached about — is Planned Parenthood!"

"It breaks my heart that when a young man is gunned down by a [police officer], the media runs with it like wildfire. Yet, if an abortionist kills a young black woman and baby, the silence itself is tragic," adds Dr. Johnny Hunter, co-founder of L.E.A.R.N.

My Uncle MLK didn't live to experience the horrors of legal abortion, which includes death to babies and harm to women. Today he would have fought just as hard to secure the rights of unborn Americans as he fought for racial justice for blacks.

Americans and all people are not racially divided biologically or spiritually, but are rather "one blood/one race." [Acts 17:26] At CRU we seek to end abortion genocide and educate and unite the human family around the sanctity of life.

We can reflect our support for life by praying, voting pro-life, and participating in the pro-life movement.

Father Frank Pavone, national director of Priests for Life, sums it up: "No other civil rights issue of our day is more important than securing the right to life for the human beings still in their mother's wombs."

Dr. Alveda C. King grew up in the civil rights movement led by her uncle, Dr. Martin Luther King Jr. She is director of African-American outreach for Priests for Life and Gospel of Life Ministries. Her family home in Birmingham, Ala., was bombed, as was her father's church office in Louisville, Ky. Alveda herself was jailed during the open housing movement. (36)

Dr. King shared with us the disturbing case of another woman that has died at the hands of an abortionist. A legally induced abortion. It is difficult to know exactly how many women have died from the procedure for several reasons. First and foremost is the fact that not all states share their abortion information with the centers for disease control.

How many abortion related deaths have occurred legally since Roe V Wade? OB/GYN Dr. Freda Bush addressed a pro-life gathering recently to discuss this. As we have already mentioned Dr. Bush noted that not all States report their abortion statistics to the CDC.

She also pointed out that both surgical and medical abortions have led to complications and death, but go unreported. Dr. Bush stated that only 45 of the 50 states in this nation report about the abortion procedure. In 2009 the CDC told us that over 400

Women's deaths due to legally induced abortions had been reported since 1973. (37)

There are more deaths due to legally induced abortions than you might think.

Life news follows the deaths of women from botched abortions and one death recorded was that of Lakisha Wilson. She was a 22-  year-old African American woman who had a late term abortion. She had been turned away from clinics in Columbus and Akron Ohio. But the clinic in Cleveland agreed to perform the procedure.

The clinic that agreed to the procedure failed to comply with the wishes of Lakisha's family. And here we discover a little known complication that also arises from abortion related deaths...Organ harvesting.

The whole abortion industry is one of the most unethical businesses in this country. We've seen on the news how a citizen journalist investigated Planned Parenthood on the subject of harvesting fetal body parts for profit. However, since the media supports Planned Parenthood we do not get an accurate account of what's happening and the persons involved in doing the investigation have been the subject of attacks themselves. (39) We'll discuss this in a later chapter, but first I want to discuss another kind of organ harvesting...the organs of the mother.

You see this kind and compassionate (sarcasm) Abortion clinic continued to perform the abortion after Lakisha's blood pressure continued to drop. By the time the procedure was complete Lakisha had stopped breathing and went into cardiac arrest. After the procedure was complete. It took the staff of the abortuary a full thirty minutes to contact an ambulance. 30 MINUTES WITH THE PATIENT IN CARDIAC ARREST AND NOT BREATHING.

EMT's noted that the patient was not breathing and that her pupils were fixed and dilated. They were unable to re-start her heart and breathing. When they got to the hospital she was given blood and placed on life support. It was decided that Lakisha was brain dead. It seems that if EMT's had been notified ASAP that Lakisha might not have suffered extensive brain damage.

Lakisha's family rushed to the hospital, not knowing the extent of the damage that had been done to their daughter. When they arrived a representative, presumably from the abortion clinic, began discussing harvesting Lakisha's organs. Before the family was completely informed as to what happened the cold and calculating "representative" begins to discuss taking their daughter's organs for transplant. WHILE THE FAMILY IS STILL IN SHOCK FROM WHAT HAPPENED TO THEIR DAUGHTER.

The family was in a state of grief and looked at this representative as the main reason that their daughter was in the condition she was in. Naturally her father was upset and wrote a note forbidding anyone to touch his daughter or take her organs.

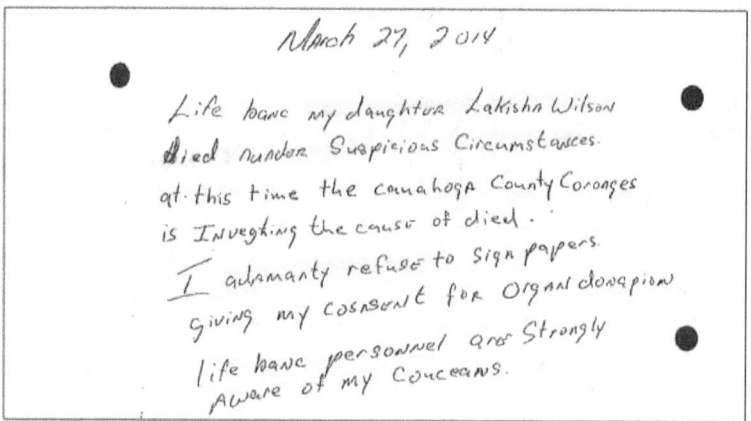

Hand-written note from Lakisha Wilson's father refusing to consent to the donation of his daughter's organs. It is dated one day before Lifebanc harvested her organs anyway.

The clinic in Cleveland had placed her pregnancy at about 19 weeks. The clinics that refused to perform the abortion had placed the pregnancy at about 23 weeks. Along with the discrepancy about the age of the ba7by there were other questions that needed to be answered.

1) How could a healthy 22-year-old die from a procedure that was supposed to be one of the safest and most common procedures in the country?
2) What went wrong and who was responsible?

Lifebanc, the company that wanted her organs, discovered that she had filled out an organ donor card and harvested her organs WITHOUT HER FAMILY'S CONSENT. Lifebanc had approached her father several times and each time he refused, which is why he wrote that hand written note.

With the organ donor card Lifebanc had a legal right to obtain Lakisha's organs and proceeded to do so. But they completely disregarded the family's wishes and violated an ethical standard in regards to this issue.

Because her organs were missing, the coroner had to conduct a partial autopsy and major questions about her death could not be answered. Without the remains of the baby the gestational age of the child could not be determined.

It was determined that Lakisha died due to insufficient oxygen to the brain but because her body was not complete at the time of the autopsy the following questions could not be answered:

1) Why had Lakisha hemorrhaged?
2) Why did the abortionist not treat her condition sooner? and:
3) Why did the clinic wait a half hour before contacting an ambulance?

This case is eerily similar to the 1978 movie coma in which patients are harvested for their organs. (40)

Of course there is no evidence that they let Lakisha die to harvest her organs, but the time it took for the clinic to contact an ambulance raises the question of whether or not there was something shady going on. We still don't have a complete answer as to why they waited a half an hour to call for help.

We mentioned the 1978 movie *Coma*. One of my favorite science fiction authors, Michael Crichton, directed the film. Though he wrote the screenplay, he didn't write the story. Author Robin Cook, who had been a friend of Crichton's, wrote the original novel on which the movie is based.

The lead is played by actress Geneviève Bujold. The studio wanted Paul Newman but Crichton fought for Bujold. The production was a star studded cast that included Michael Douglas, Rip Torn, Richard Widmark, Tom Selleck, Joanna Kerns, and Ed Harris, among others.

In the story (spoilers) Dr. Susan Wheeler (Bujold) is devastated when her friend is declared brain dead after minor surgery. The doctor comes across a similar situation that happened to another patient at the same hospital (Boston memorial.) Upon further investigation she discovers that there were many patients that wound up dying under similar circumstances.

All of the deaths take place in the same operating room and the bodies all wind up going to the same mysterious company: The Jefferson Institute. The patients are being rendered brain dead by use of carbon monoxide poisoning. When the good doctor finds this out the killer attempts to poison her but his plans are thwarted. (41)

As I think about this movie and the similarities to this and other cases, I wonder if this could be a case of life imitating art? To what degree will the U.S. news media stay silent? There was, after all, an appalling lack of interest in the Kermit Gosnell case by the mainstream media.

When women died of illegally induced abortions the media ran with those stories. When women die from legally induced abortions the media stays silent. Don't those women's lives matter? The truth is that it's not about women's lives, but rather it's about politics.

Why do Pro-choice advocates oppose parental notification laws? A child cannot have her ear pierced without permission from his/her parents but yet a young girl can have her uterus pierced without telling her parents? Does anyone else find this to be wrong?

40

Another case I want to bring to your attention in this volume is the story of 18-year-old Marla Cardamone, mother of one:

When Marla found herself pregnant with a child she hadn't planned she was set on putting that child up for adoption, it is alleged that she was on medication; Tegretol and Elavil. A medical social worker talked to her about an abortion. She told Marla that the fetus would be damaged because of the medication. Although there was a 92% chance that there was nothing wrong with the baby.

Marla entered the hospital on august 15, 1989. Marla's medical condition was such that the organic compound urea should not have been used. However, that compound was injected into her uterus anyway. Some mishap during the procedure caused a reaction called generalized necrosis. The laminaria was also inserted in such a way as to cause septicemia, and massive cortical necrosis of the kidneys.

Needless to say Marla got sick that night with nausea, vomiting and involuntary urination.

6:30 am: A charge nurse contacted the first of several doctors that would treat her, but no cultures were taken.

7:00 am: Marla was becoming increasingly disoriented and her speech patterns were off.

7:15 am: Marla's blood pressure was 80/40 and her pulse was off at 144. She wasn't responding, grunting loudly and having seizures.

10:00 am: antibiotics were administered intravenously.

12:15 pm: Marla died from septicemia.

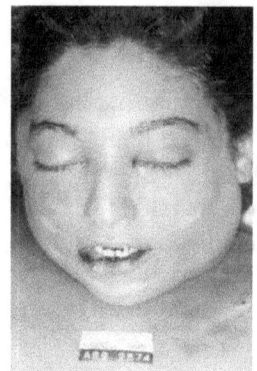

Marla's family sued the clinic for failure to notify them of her condition as it deteriorated. Marla's parents adopted her only child. In the lawsuit the doctor and clinic were faulted for psychiatrically contraindicated abortion, failure to evacuate the dead fetus also for an overdose of Pitocin, and failure to consult qualified doctors.

Marla's mother added with a note of bitterness: "I had to file a lawsuit to get any answers. Marla had died of septicemia--a massive infection from the abortion. I also learned that the social worker had never seen Marla's sonogram or discussed the results with her. Marla never saw the words on the sonogram report that would have changed everything: *No abnormalities detected.* My daughter was pressured to have an abortion, and there had been no reason for it, no reason at all.

I've often wondered why pro-choice women's groups have never expressed any sympathy or concern over Marla's death. Why aren't they demanding justice? Why aren't they concerned that Marla was lied to about the condition of her baby and wasn't shown the sonogram results? Why aren't they concerned that proper treatment was delayed because Marla was misdiagnosed by a resident who was only two months out of medical school? Why are they so quiet?

I believe it's because pro-choice groups don't want women to read or hear about abortion injuries and deaths. Bad publicity hurts their cause. That's why they prefer that Marla and her baby remain hidden statistics." (42)

So here we have a clear case of a woman who had already opted for adoption, who was coerced into having an abortion that she didn't want with medication administered by someone who wasn't qualified to administer it. And they kept vital information away from her concerning the development of the baby she was carrying. Where were the pro-choicers while her rights were being violated? Supporting her attackers of course.

Again while common sense laws are being passed to try to protect women from such incidents as the aforementioned from happening the very people who claim to be supporting her rights are trying to strike down these self-same laws. Where is the news media when these flagrant violations of human rights are taking place? Supporting those who attacked Marla. A conspiracy of silence is taking place all in the name of liberal politics.

Earlier we discussed the case of Gerri Santoro who died of an illegally induced abortion in 1964. The media played up her death for the sake of liberal politics and to justify legalizing the procedure. But now I want to discuss the case of Erika Peterson who died from a legally induced abortion in 1961. Here is a clear case of media bias once again. The fact is that Santoro could have sought a legal abortion in 1964 in certain states, as Erika Peterson did. The fact is that the media didn't care about either women as they used Santoro's death to political advantage while ignoring Peterson's death because they couldn't use said death to any political gain.

What about medically induced abortions? Have they led to any deaths? Apparently there are about 12 deaths known to have been caused by medically induced abortions worldwide with seven of them occurring in the U.S. I am not that familiar with these cases so I will simply quote the statistics here. Though percentage wise this may not seem like a lot of deaths when you consider the number of women seeking this type of abortion it is important to note that none of these women needed to die.

Eight Medical Abortion Deaths in U.S. Women from Sepsis

United States: 8 (eight) deaths were associated with sepsis (serious infection involving the bloodstream following medical abortion with mifepristone and misoprostol. All but one fatal sepsis case reported vaginal misoprostol use; buccal misoprostol use was reported in one case. FDA has concluded the deaths from these infections may possibly be related to the use of mifepristone and misoprostol for medical abortion. [2] [4] [5] [6] [7]

Seven cases tested positive for Clostridium sordellii toxic shock syndrome following medical abortion:

- 2009-July 28, a 21-year-old previously healthy White woman (name unknown), 7 weeks (49 days) gestation, died 12 days after initiation of medical abortion.

- 2008-August 18, a 29-year-old White Hispanic woman (name unknown), 5 weeks (35 days) gestation, died 6 days after initiation of medical abortion.

- 2007-July 4, a 18-year-old previously healthy woman (name unknown), 6.5 weeks gestation (46 days), died approximately 8 days after initiation of medical abortion. Patient was administered 200 mg oral mifepristone and 800 mcg buccal misoprostol.

- 2005-June 14, a 34-year-old previously healthy White woman, Oriane Shevin, 45 days' gestation, died approximately 4 days after initiation of medical abortion.

- 2004-January 14, a 22-year-old previously healthy African American woman, Chanelle Bryant, 53 days' gestation, died approximately 6 days after initiation of medical abortion.

- 2003-December 29, a 21-year-old previously healthy Asian woman, Hoa Thuy "Vivian" Tran, 43 days' gestation, died 5 days after initiation of medical abortion.

- 2003-September 17, a 18-year-old previously healthy White woman, Holly Patterson, 47 days gestation, died 7 days after initiation of medical abortion.

One case tested positive for fatal Clostridium perfringens infection:

- 2006-March 9, a 24-year-old previously healthy woman (name unknown), 8.5 weeks' gestation, died 7 days after initiation of medical abortion. (43)

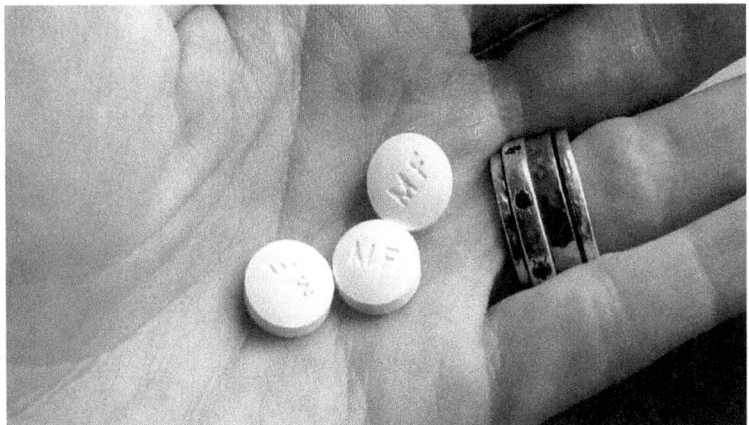

These pills look so innocent while being held in someone's hand. How healthy are they? For the aforementioned women they were deadly.

Holly Patterson died from medical abortion

Elizabeth Cady Stanton. It may not be fair to try to categorize early feminists as "pro-life" or "pro-choice." But their writings clearly opposed the practice of abortion.

Elizabeth Blackwell, the first woman to obtain a medical degree in America.

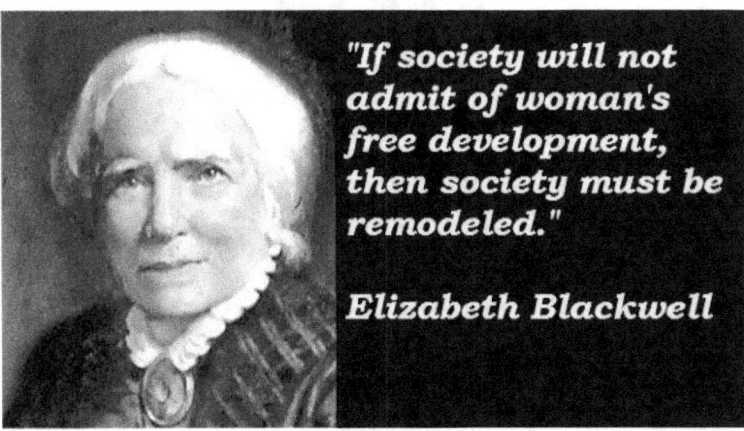

"If society will not admit of woman's free development, then society must be remodeled."

Elizabeth Blackwell

OFFICIAL FIRST DAY COVER

Hobart &
William Smith
Colleges

Honoring GENEVA MEDICAL COLLEGE

Elizabeth Blackwell, M.D.
1821–1910
FIRST WOMAN M.D. IN AMERICA
GRADUATED JANUARY 23, 1849

The first woman to achieve a degree in medicine also wrote
against abortion.

The first woman to run for President, in an age when women couldn't vote. Her views on abortion widely contradict Hilary Clintons.

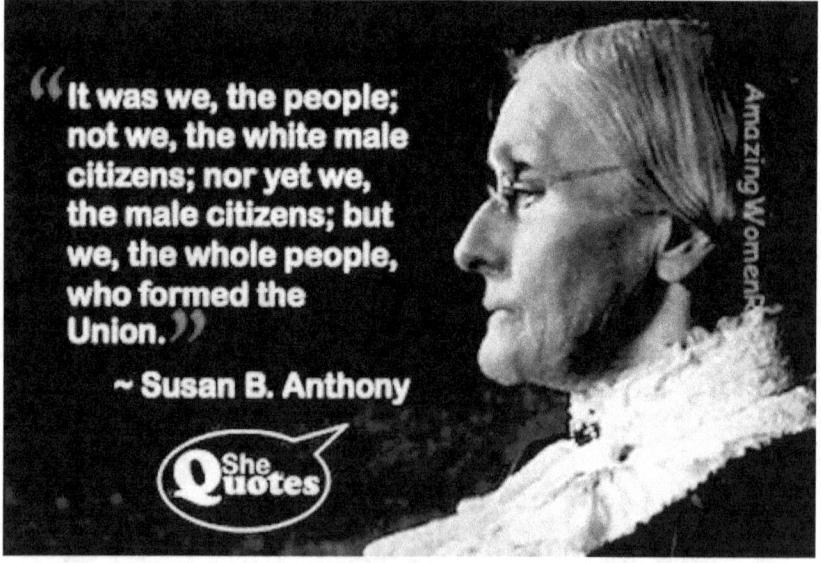

Susan B. Anthony. Her quotes on abortion would not be appreciated by today's feminist in the *NOW* organization. Her views would be more akin to the *Feminists for Life* organization.

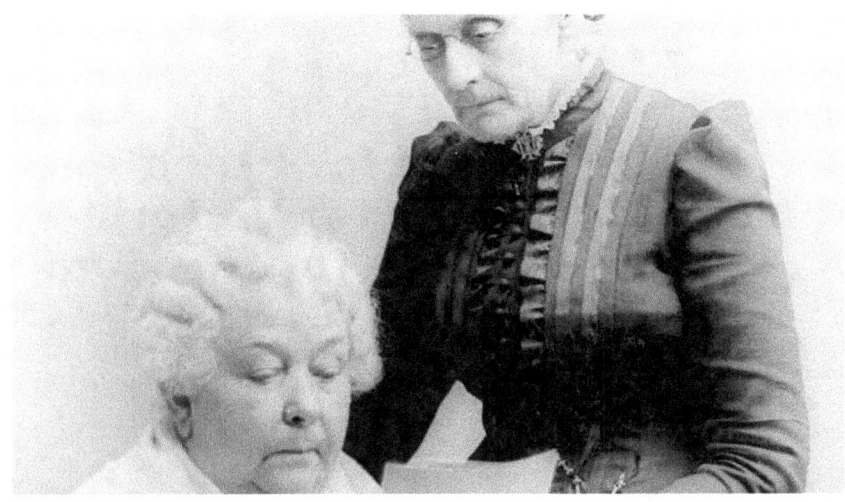

Susan B. Anthony and Elizabeth Cady Stanton.

Victoria Woodhill, the first woman to run for President also
wrote against the practice of abortion.

**Woodull for President!
a vote for Victoria
is a vote for freedom**

1872 - EQUAL RIGHTS PARTY - 2012

6

The Attackers

Now let's look at the people who are waging the *war on women*. We've seen that there are real casualties in this war. There are babies who have survived the war and lived to tell the tale. There are women who were lulled into a false feeling of confidence that nothing would go wrong with the "procedure" only to lose their lives. And finally there is an organization performing medical "procedures" that do not have to adhere to the same standards as those who are providing real health care thanks to the Supreme Court of the United States. But who are these abortionists that are allowed to attack women and get away with it? Let's start with the most notorious one of all.

Kermit Gosnell

This monster had been killing live babies that survived his abortion "procedure" for over thirty years. It is estimated that over 1,000 live late term babies have been destroyed at his hands. How was he allowed to continue his practice for so long? and how was he finally brought down?

Gosnell owned and operated a clinic in Philadelphia called the *Women's Medical Society*. In 2011 Gosnell was charged with 8 counts of murder, 24 felony accounts of performing abortions beyond the 24-week limit as required by Pennsylvania law, 227 misdemeanor counts of violating the 24-hour consent law and numerous other violations. It really sickens me that this man was able to skirt the law for so long. Because Planned Parenthood is so protected by the media in this country and because they donate vast amounts of money to politicians and political groups their clinics go virtually un-policed and the authorities, for the most part, look the other way.

When did Gosnell begin his practice? He was born in 1941 and was a top student at Central High School where he graduated from in 1959. He attended Dickinson College then moved on to Jefferson Medical School where he received his degree in 1966.

In the early days he actually performed some good in his life including opening the Mantua halfway house, a halfway house for drug addicts in West Philadelphia. By the end of the '60's he became a proponent of abortion rights and has actually had the gall to say "as a physician, I am very concerned about the sanctity of life. But it is for this precise reason that I provide abortions for women who want and need them." (45)

He had performed fifteen second trimester abortions that were televised using an experimental *super coil* method. This method caused complications in nine of the women including severe complications in some. Many called this procedure the "Mother's Day Massacre." (46)

By 2011 Gosnell had the reputation of performing abortions on poor and immigrant women. He charged anywhere from $1,600 to $3,000 for late term abortions. He also practiced in other states like Delaware and Louisiana. So his reign of terror was not resigned to just one state. It was at the clinic in Louisiana that Gosnell recruited employees for his operation in Philadelphia.

Complaints about Gosnell go as far back as 1989. *From Wikipedia*:

- 1989 and 1993 – cited by Pennsylvania Department of Health for having no nurses in the recovery room.

- 1996 – censured and fined in both Pennsylvania and New York states, for employing unlicensed personnel.

- Around 1996 – Pediatrician Dr Schwartz – the former head of adolescent services at the Children's Hospital of Philadelphia and as of 2010, Philadelphia's health commissioner – testified in the 2010 hearing that around 1996 or 1997, he had hand-delivered a letter of complaint about Gosnell's practice to the Secretary of Health's office and stopped referring patients to the clinic, but *received no response.*

- 2000 – Civil lawsuit filed on behalf of the children of Semika Shaw, who had called the clinic the day after an abortion to report heavy bleeding, and died 3 days later of a perforated uterus and a bloodstream infection. The case alleged that Gosnell had failed to tell her to return to the clinic or seek emergency medical care. It was settled out of court in 2002 for $900,000.

- Around 2001 – Gosnell claimed to be providing children's vaccines under a program administered by the Health Department's Division of Disease Control, but was repeatedly suspended for failing to maintain logs and for storing vaccines in unsanitary and inappropriate refrigerators, and at improper temperatures.

- December 2001 – ex-employee Marcella Choung gave what the Grand Jury would later call "a detailed written complaint" to the Pennsylvania Department of State, one which she followed up with an interview in March 2002.

- 2006 – Civil lawsuit filed by patient but dismissed as out of time. The complaint was that Gosnell had been unable to complete an abortion, but then apparently failed or refused to call paramedics or other clinical emergency personnel, after the patient had needed help. The patient reported, "I really felt like he was going to let me die."

In total during the course of his career, 46 known lawsuits had been filed against Gosnell over some 32 years. Observers claimed that there was a *complete failure by Pennsylvania regulators* who had overlooked other repeated concerns brought to their attention, including lack of trained staff, "barbaric" conditions, and a high level of illegal late-term abortions.

55

So, finally, after more than thirty years of killing women and

babies, something was done. After months of investigation by the DEA and the Philadelphia police dept. on February 18, 2010, the FBI granted a search warrant for Gosnell's house of horrors and a raid ensued. Perhaps if they hadn't ignored earlier complaints Karnamaya Mongar might still be alive.

Karnamaya Mongar

This unfortunate woman sought a "safe and legal" abortion at Gosnell's clinic in 2009. She was a refugee from Bhutan. She had survived about 20 years in a refugee camp. Karnamaya was not a weak woman. But then she entered Kermit Gosnell's house of horrors, another casualty in the *war on women*.

Mrs. Mongar signed the proper forms (which she couldn't read) and then was doped up by unauthorized employees of the clinic. But of course, abortion clinics don't have to follow the same guidelines as others in the medical community. The staff at Gosnell's clinic gave her repeated doses of Demerol, a sedative that isn't used widely today because of the dangers involved. But the good doctor liked it because it was cheap. The drug wasn't monitored or recorded. She stopped breathing. No one noticed for an undetermined amount of time.

Gosnell was finally called in and tried to do CPR. However, *his defibrillator was broken!* This wonderful humanitarian (sarcasm) also did not try to administer emergency medications that might have restarted her heart. (48)

Now, I ask you, where were the feminists and liberals while this was going on? Why, they were supporting her attacker of course. We shouldn't place undue burdens on women by forcing abortion clinics to adhere to the same guidelines as other medical professionals. We should allow these doctors to keep lifesaving equipment like *broken defibrillators*.

Gosnell's horror clinic. Babies died here on a weekly basis and I don't mean before they were born. The good doctor broke newborn's spines with scissors to kill them.

This headline should have graced every major newspaper in the country, instead the media almost completely ignored this story.

Where was the media when America's most prolific serial killer was being tried for his crimes? Not at the trial. Here is the media section of the court room. How could any journalist know about this case and ignore it, then live with themselves?

Another view of Gosnell's horror hospital.

Looking at this picture of the front window to Gosnell's clinic I'm reminded of the old universal horror films with an ominous tone.

Unsanitary medical equipment and more victims of Kermit Gosnell in plastic bags. There are other horrifying pictures of babies that I will not show in this book.

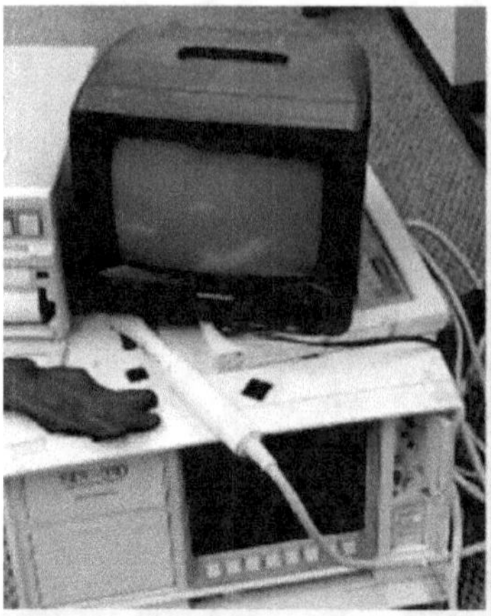

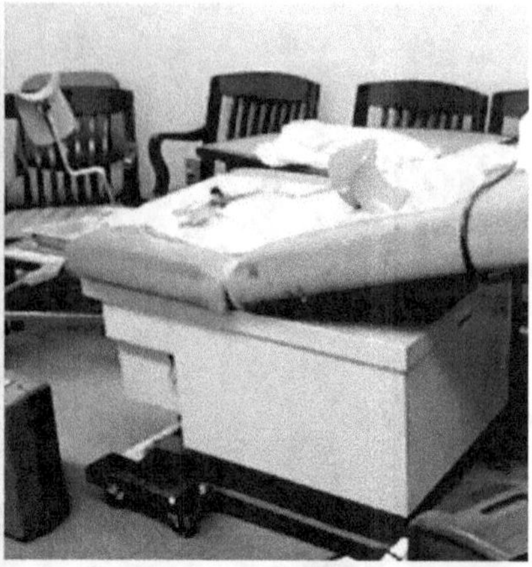

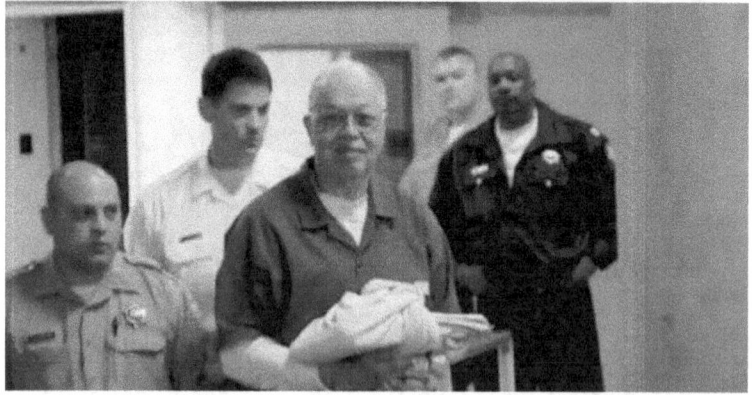

More unsanitary equipment at the clinic and finally the monster
is being led to his fate. He has a smug look on his face.

What we've just discussed is only the beginning of what went on in that abortuary:

1) Clinic employee Steven Massof claims that over 100 babies had their spines "snipped" after being born alive.

2) Writing fraudulent prescriptions for thousands of pills including Xanax, Percocet and OxyContin among others.

3) A fifteen-year-old girl told the good doctor that she changed her mind and didn't want an abortion. She was then restrained against her will and forced into the abortion while the good doctor told her that this is the same care he would give his own daughter (be glad you're not his daughter.

4) A 28-year-old woman who experienced such pain that she couldn't walk. She returned to the clinic with portions of her baby still inside her. The abortion was completed *without anesthesia*!

5) Another fifteen-year-old girl given an abortion without parental permission.

6) Pennsylvania state officials failed to visit Gosnell's abortuary since 1993. It was discovered in 2011 that none of the State's 22 Abortuary's had been visited for more 15 years.

It was decided under the governorship of liberal Tom Ridge that inspecting these clinics somehow caused an undue burden on women that seek abortion. MAKING SURE THAT THESE TORTURE CHAMBERS COMPLIED WITH PROPER MEDICAL STANDARDS CONSTITUTES AN UNDUE BURDON ON WOMEN!!!!

How do these news journalists and politicians even live with themselves? How can they know of an important news story such as this where unhealthy practices were going on and even led to death and murder for more than thirty years? (48)

Every time a crackpot shoots people at an abortuary it makes front page news and the media is all over it. It doesn't just make local news it is discussed for weeks and they try to link these crack pots to pro-life groups, yet horror stories like Gosnell's go unreported for the most part. I keep wondering how these people who attack women on a daily basis are protected by the government and the media.

From Wikipedia:

Criticism of media coverage

A perception had built up among some journalists and pro-life groups that there had been a reluctance to report on the trial among mainstream media. In an April 11, 2013 opinion column for USA Today, Kirsten Powers wrote: "A Lexis-Nexis search shows none of the news shows on the three major national television networks has mentioned the Gosnell trial in the last three months", and that national press coverage was represented by a Wall Street Journal columnist who "hijacked" a segment on Meet the Press, a single page A-17 story on the first day of the trial by The New York Times, and no original coverage by The Washington Post.

While Kirsten Powers is credited by some for drawing media coverage to the Gosnell trial, Dave Weigel at Slate.com reported it was **conservatives' aggressive use of social media, especially Twitter** (*activism and social media works wonders in today's society* – **RK**), that "goaded" the press into covering the trial in Philadelphia. According to Weigel, Troy Newman, president of the Kansas-based pro-life Operation Rescue, had organized a Twitter campaign using "#Gosnell" to break the "Gosnell Media Blackout." Key to that social media campaign was a picture of rows of empty media seats in the Gosnell courtroom taken by Calkins Media columnist J.D. Mullane.

Mullane told Weigel he was struck by the absence of media at the trial, and took out his iPhone and snapped the picture, Tweeting it later that night.

"Mullane retweeted the photo a few more times, with different captions, because it had been packed into a snowball (of criticism)" which included Powers' column for USA Today, Weigel wrote. The empty seats photograph was used by pro-life activists to show "proof" of media dereliction. Weigel wrote: "It worked. An estimated 106,000 #Gosnell tweets later, on April 15, Mullane reported that major networks and newspapers had sent their reporters to cover the trial—Fox News, the New York Times, the Washington Post."

Writing for The Washington Post, Melinda Henneberger responded that "we didn't write more because *the only abortion story most outlets ever cover in the news pages is every single threat or perceived threat to abortion rights* (italics mine – RK.) In fact, that is so fixed a view of what constitutes coverage of that issue that it's genuinely hard, I think, for many journalists to see a story outside that paradigm as news. That's not so much a <u>conscious decision</u> as a <u>reflex</u>, but *the effect is one-sided coverage*". Explaining why some of her colleagues did not report on the story, Henneberger wrote, "One colleague viewed Gosnell's alleged atrocities as a local crime story, though I can't think of another mass murder, with hundreds of victims, that we ever saw that way. Another said it was just too lurid, though that didn't keep us from covering Jeffrey Dahmer, or that aspiring cannibal at the NYPD."[143] Writing for Bloomberg View, Jeffrey Goldberg said that this story "upsets a particular narrative about the reality of certain types of abortion, and that reality isn't something some pro-choice absolutists want to discuss."

The Los Angeles Times, The Atlantic, Slate, and Time all published opinion columns where the writer thought the incident was not getting as much media coverage as it deserved. Megan McArdle explains that she didn't cover it because it made her ill, but also how being pro-choice influenced writers saying "most of us tend to be less interested in sick-making stories if the sick-making was done by 'our side,'" saying, "this story should have been covered much more than it was — covered as a national policy issue, not a 'local crime story.'" Martin Baron, The Post's executive editor, claims he wasn't aware of the story until Thursday, 11 April, when readers began emailing him about it, saying "I wish I could be conscious of all stories everywhere, but I can't be". They ultimately decided that, in fact, the story warranted attention because of "the seriousness and scope of the alleged crimes and because this was a case that resonated in policy arguments and national politics", adding "In retrospect, we regret not having staffed the trial sooner. But, as you know, we don't have unlimited resources, and [...] there is a lot of competition for our staff's attention". He insisted that "we never decide what to cover for ideological reasons, no matter what critics might claim. Accusations of ideological motives are easy to make, even if they're not supported by the facts". The New York Times also acknowledged the lack of coverage and reported on the online campaign and subsequent increase in coverage of the case. While Powers' piece clearly sparked debate among journalists, Katherine Bindley also highlights contrasting views, as does Paul Farhi. A column on Salon.com questioned whether the Gosnell case was an example of liberal media bias, saying that conservative media and politicians had also given little attention to the story until April 2013.

In April 2013, 71 other Members of Congress joined Congresswoman Marsha Blackburn in a letter condemning the media "blackout" on the Gosnell trial. (48)

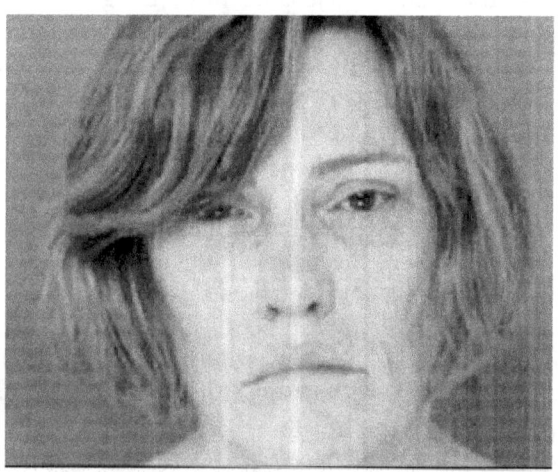

What does accused PA murderer Kermit Gosnell and a troubled Louisiana abortion clinic have in common? Eileen O'Neill, who once worked for Delta Clinic of Baton Rouge. She was arrested with Gosnell and charged for theft, consipracy, racketeering, perjury, and false writing. Conditions at the Delta Clinic mirror conditions at Gosnell's "house of horrors."

Gosnell isn't alone. There are more like him in the good ol' U.S.A.

The Movie:

Q) What movie project raised the most funds on the Indiegogo site?

A) The film that's currently in post-production about the serial killer Kermit Gosnell.

The Indiegogo site has raised more than 2 million dollars as of this writing and has some high profile Hollywood types in the cast and crew including *Lois and Clark* star Dean Cane.

The film makers are Phelim McAleer, Ann McElhinney and Magda Segieda. They have faced numerous obstacle's in their effort including censorship from the Kickstarter campaign, another crowd funding site. When Kickstarter refused to allow them to seek funds they went to Indiegogo. Their crowdfunding goals were made and the cast and crew are mostly in place but they are still taking donations to try and give as good a production as they can. (49)

The Writers on the Gosnell movie project include Andrew Klavan and Phelim McAleer. Klavan has impressive credits to his name. He's an author who's had two of his novels adapted for the silver screen *True Crime* (1999) and *Don't Say a Word* (2001.) He's a two times Edgar award winner (nominated four times) and has worked on other films like *White of the Eye* (1987) and *A Shock to the System*.

Klavan began as a script reader for Columbia pictures and worked in radio for a time. He's a self-avowed conservative and has his own podcast: *The Andrew Klavan show* which is heard on the conservative web site *The Daily Wire*. (51)

The director is Nick Searcy who also appears in the film as Mike Cohen. His credits include the FX series *Justified*. He played Deke Slayton in the Tom Hanks miniseries *From the Earth to the Moon*. He's also been in *Days of Thunder, The Fugitive* and *Moneyball*. On Television he can be seen in *Archer* (sort of,) *American Gothic*, and *The Real McCoy*.

Dean Cain stars as Detective James Wood. We know Cain from his role as Superman in the Television series *Lois and Clark: The New Adventures of Superman*. He also hosted *Ripley's Believe it or Not* and appeared in the soap opera *Hit the Floor*. He also appeared in the films *Militia, Out of Time*, and *Heaven's Door*.

Also appearing in this film are Michael Beach (*Lean on Me, One False Move,*) Sarah Jane Morris (*Seven Pounds, Coyote Ugly*) and Darryl Cox (*Robocop, JFK*) The cast is impressive for an independent film, but who is playing Kermit Gosnell?

Enter Earl Billings. Billings has a long and dignified career in film and television. He was best known for the TV series *What's Happening* and had roles in such films as *Antwon Fisher, Fat Albert* and *Bustin' Loose*.

Even though the producers have raised more than they need. There's always room for more. The more money they make the better the film will be. If you would like to donate to this exceptional project, go the Indiegogo site. (52)

This is from the producers on the Indiegogo web site:

Today we want to share with you the news about a great opportunity we've been given. Indiegogo has just extended an invitation to us to join their pilot program called "Forever Funding". It allows projects to re-open their crowdfunding campaign and continue raising funds.

There are 3 big reasons why we are very excited about this:
After our Indiegogo campaign closed, we received many messages from people who missed the deadline but still wanted to contribute to the project. Now, they will be able to do it online in a safe, straight forward manner and claim their reward.

We cannot emphasize enough the positive feedback we received from potential distributors of the Gosnell Movie. They saw the 26,574 contributors as a living proof that this movie has a highly motivated audience who will watch it and spread the word about it. Their excitement will grow proportionally as the number of supporters grow! We want to secure distribution for the Gosnell

Movie prior to or during filming and being able to show a big number of backers on our Indiegogo page will be a huge help in our negotiations.

The truth is that our budget is extremely tight. We asked for $2.1m in an all-or-nothing campaign and we absolutely can and will make a movie for that amount. But given the scope and importance of the story, we cannot help but imagine what this movie could be with a little more help.

Based on the three reasons above, we're re-opening this campaign with a clear purpose. Here are our stretch goals that we are hoping to reach, and you can help us get there:

Over 100,000 backers – This is very possible. Imagine if each of you found 3 friends and got them to contribute just ONE DOLLAR. Here is the math: 3 friend's x 26,574 + 26,574 of you = 106,296. This would be an amazingly powerful statement of support and a message to distributors that there is a big audience wanting this movie to be seen!

Another $300,000 to extend the shooting schedule – Right now we have enough funds for a three week shoot. That's the absolute minimum we need and we'll be under a lot of pressure to fit everything into this timeframe. With these additional funds, we would be able to film for one more week, which would allow us to construct more powerful in-depth scenes and let our director and actors give their best performances.

Another $200,000 for the actors – in low budget movies like ours, most of the funds go to "below the line", fixed-cost necessities, such as equipment, filming crew and locations. What remains, can be spent on the "talent" - the actors, and those remaining funds dictate who you can hire. If you enjoy watching movies, you know well what difference a very talented actor can make on screen – it's invaluable! You can help us take a step up with the actors we hire and make the Gosnell Movie even better.

We can do this together! Veronica Mars, a teen detective movie that asked for $2.1m, raised $5.7m, we think the Gosnell Movie is more important, we hope you do too. A guy in Ohio posted a photo of a potato salad and raised $55,492... to make potato salad. We love a good potato salad ourselves, but we think the Gosnell Movie is more important, we hope you do too.

Please remember that every single dollar counts, every new contributor adds to our success. You can use whatever tools you like best: Facebook, Twitter, email, phone – to spread the word about our new effort.

THANK YOU. (52)

Earl Billings as Dr. Kermit Gosnell

A still from the movie: *Gosnell*. Coming soon to a theatre near you.

Dean Cane plays Detective James Wood, who investigated the
good doctor.

Nick Searcy is directing the film and also has a role.

The actual house of horrors.

Screen writer Andrew Klavan.

Abu Hayat

Meet the man that tore Ana Rosa Rodriguez right arm off and proclaimed his innocence during the trial that saw him do serious time for his offense. The "pro-choice" camp is continuously talking about the need for "safe and legal" abortion to get rid of "back alley" abortionists. But the fact is that the same people who performed abortions before legalization in 1973 are the same people who are performing abortions today. We'll look at the statistics later but right now I want to discuss another hidden statistic, Sophia McCoy.

Another great crusader of women's rights (sarcasm, again) Abu Hayat, who deserves just as big a page on Wikipedia as Kermit Gosnell, but doesn't have it, has probably done just as much damage as Gosnell. Shortly before he maimed Ana Rosa for life, attacking both her and her mother, Hayat attacked another 17-year-old girl named Sophia McCoy.

The High School student sought out Hayat's services in September of 1990. After the procedure, on the 19th of September, Sophia was brought to King's County Hospital complaining of pain and shortness of breath. She had vaginal bleeding. Her mother had taken her to Dr. Hayat's clinic the day before. When she did a standard follow up call the good doctor denied that he had touched her.

A panel of two doctors and a lay person by the State Board of Professional Conduct was convened to discuss Sophia's case. Dr.

73

Patricia Harding testified before the panel. She told the panel that dirty instruments were probably used on the young girl. Once again common sense laws about proper care and treatment might have saved this girls life and once again "pro-choice" forces claim that having an abortion doctor adhere to the same standards as other medical professionals is somehow "punishing women" and "undermining *Roe V. Wade.*"

Dr. Hayat himself did not attend the hearings which the board described as a "flagrant disregard" for the panel. Hayat's lawyers claimed that they needed more time to prepare and wanted the hearings postponed until they were ready. Many others testified before the panel that they had suffered at the hands of Hayat. (53)

And before anyone says that Hayat was a lone practice back alley abortionist it should be noted that he was a member of the *National Abortion Federation* which supposedly has only the finest physicians within their organization. From their website:

"What is a NAF Clinic? NAF is the professional association of abortion providers in North America. .... In order to become a member, a clinic must complete a rigorous application process. Member clinics have agreed to comply with our standards for quality and care.... NAF periodically conducts site visits to confirm that our clinics are in compliance with our guidelines.

They must have been too busy to make sure that Hayat's clinic complied with their standards. Hayat had been recommended to Sophia's mother by someone that is anonymous to "the Willoughby Avenue Clinic." She was kept for about 4 hours then discharged with a prescription for anti-biotics.

After Sophia was brought to the hospital she was treated by Dr. Harding and it was discovered that she had a perforated uterus and serious sepsis. An emergency hysterectomy was performed but it was too late. Sophia died on September 26, 1990. Leaving behind a one-year-old son.

As we've seen, the great humanitarian member of the National Abortion Federation at first denied touching her. Then when Sophia's mother identified him he tried to tell the physicians that Sophia had expelled a fetus at home and came to him for help at which point he had sent her to the hospital. (54)

The findings were reported to Mario Cuomo's District Attorney and the *New York Health Department* but *nothing was done about it* until Hayat tore off Ana Rosa's arm more than a year later. Of course nothing was done about it, that would have punished women and undermined *Roe V. Wade* somehow.

I want you to understand that this was not just one case but many others have died at his hands and reported substandard care. 8 women, including Clara Robles-Veliz had filed complaints about the good doctor. Dr. Hayat never responded to Clara's suit and was found guilty by default. He appealed the decision but the authorities let it stand. At that point Hayat declared bankruptcy when he couldn't afford, or didn't want, to pay his bills. The man had no malpractice insurance.

The authorities in New York completely ignored all of those complaints, which had gone as far back as 1988. If they had acted sooner than Ana Rosa may have been able to keep both of her arms and Sophia might be alive today. (55)

with attempting an illegal third-trimester
Supreme Court in Manhattan yesterday.

The good doctor was finally sentenced to between 9 and 29 years in prison. His lawyer called the penalty a death sentence for his client. He was the first person since 1981 that was convicted for violating the state's law prohibiting the procedure after the 24th week.

The good doctor was also found guilty of assault against patient Marie Moise, and falsifying records to cover his actions. After sentencing Hayat proclaimed his innocence to the Judge. (56)

Why do these monsters think that they can get away, literally, with murder? What can cause them to be so calloused and careless with this procedure that caused more than 400 women that we know of to have died from legally induced abortion? The answer lies in one of the first court trials against an abortionist that killed a baby after the babies live birth.

Daytona Beach Morning Journal - Dec 18, 1976   Browse thi

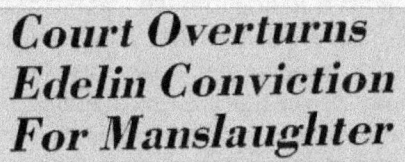

Court Overturns Edelin Conviction For Manslaughter

BOSTON (AP) — The Massachusetts Supreme Court Friday overturned the manslaughter conviction of Dr. Kenneth C. Edelin in the death of a fetus during a legal abortion. The landmark case had made physicians across the country reluctant to perform abortions after the first three months of pregnancy.

"It's been a long time getting to this day," Edelin told a news conference.

"This decision will relieve physicians in general who worry about sound medical judgments ending up as a criminal case," said Edelin, assistant director of obstetrics and gynecology at Boston City Hospital.

The state Supreme Court overturned his Feb. 15, 1975, conviction, saying Edelin had "no evil frame of mind, was actuated by no criminal purpose and committed no wanton or reckless act in carrying out the medical procedures on Oct 3, 1973."

The prosecution at Edelin's trial had claimed he tried to asphyxiate the fetus inside the mother and did not try to save it after it was removed. Edelin's defense had argued the fetus died before birth.

"I feel fantastic, overjoyed — what else can I say?" Edelin told reporters in the office of his lawyer, William P Homans Jr. "It really feels good to be able to smile for a change. It's been extremely difficult over the last 2½

DR. KENNETH C. EDELIN   (See EDELIN on Page 3A)

Edelin—
(Continued from Page 1A)

years. Today is just a fantastic day."

The abortion of a 20 to 24 week old male fetus of a 17 year old unmarried woman occurred after the U S Supreme Court legalized abortions but before Massachusetts enacted a new law of its own.

The state supreme court concurred in Edelin's defense that his prosecution was tantamount to the state second guessing a physician's professional judgment.

"The manslaughter statute is flat, and it would be not only incongruous but, we think, unconstitutional to attempt to bring it to bear on a physician as he went about the predelivery process of performing an abortion," said the decision by Justice Benjamin Kaplan. "Of course, manslaughter could not be supported by proof merely of a mistake of judgment, even if that was the result of negligence or gross negligence."

The jury had been told it could convict Edelin only on the basis of actions he took after the birth. "Taking the evidence on this point   we find nothing of substance in it to permit a submission to a jury as to criminal 'recklessness' or the like," the Supreme Court said.

"To all appearances, the fetus was dead Dr. Edelin found no heartbeat and saw no other indication that he had a living being in his hands Manslaughter assumes the victim was a live and independent person," the court said

The Supreme Court said the fetus may have been alive "in the very narrow sense that there was some postnatal gasping of air as revealed by microscopic analysis," but was dead to all appearances

Homans said under the abortion law the state has since enacted, Edelin's action probably would be considered legal.

The man in question is Dr. Kenneth C. Edelin an OB/GYN who performed an abortion on a 17-year-old girl in 1973. He is the first known abortionist that killed a baby after live birth. He went to trial in 1975. The deck was stacked against the prosecutor from the get go. The attorney could not use terms like "murder," "Suffocate," "Suffocation," or "Baby boy" (even though the baby he killed was a boy.) (57)

The baby in question was 20 to 24 weeks in development when Edelin ended his life outside of his mother's womb. At the time he was thirty-six years old and said of his first trial: "I don't believe it's possible for a jury of people like those who were selected to really understand the issues, especially some of the scientific and medical problems encountered at the trial, we attempted to educate them, and I guess we failed. As a jury of my peers...it certainly was not."

So basically he was saying that the jury was a bunch of dumb yokels who wouldn't know what a baby was if they held one. What scientific and medical problems was Edelin talking about? Since the baby was between 20 and 24 weeks, let's take a look at what a baby looks like in the middle. Here's a baby born prematurely (note: this is not the same baby that he was accused of killing.) and survived at 22 weeks the dumb yokels actually thought this was a baby.

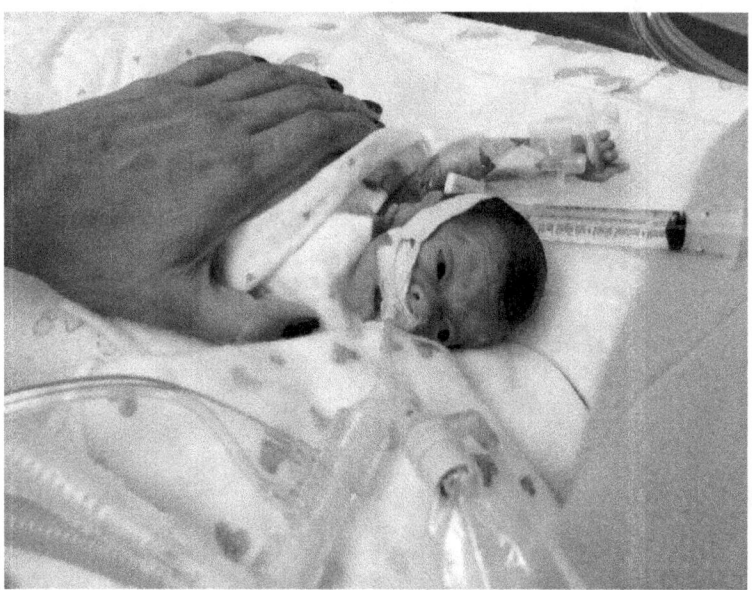

Now, I ask you, could you hold that baby's nose until it stopped breathing? Was this a human being? Should a man who takes this life have done jail time? The first jury convicted Edelin for taking a human life but he was later acquitted on appeal.

Even Edelin agrees that this was a baby. Here's the statement he made about the abortion after it was complete: "I will continue to do abortions. They are a woman's right," he said after his conviction, "Women since they've been on this earth have been making that choice, whether they want to carry that **_baby_** or not.... The only humane thing we can do is make sure that when they make that choice they have the opportunity to make it under the best conditions possible."

So the judge in the first trial wouldn't allow the prosecutor to use the term "baby boy," even though Edelin used that precise term to describe the child that he killed. Tell me Dr. Edelin, what do you propose we do with the baby if she chooses not to carry it? Get rid of it? How can you get rid of a baby? Is that the humane thing to do?

Just like with Gianna Jessen, whom we've discussed earlier, Edelin tried to kill the baby with a saline abortion, another saline abortion that failed and led to the _dreaded complication_ that liberals hate: A baby born alive.

"Defense Attorney Homans called this reasoning 'metaphysical.' He argued that the entire operation, including the death of the fetus, was protected by the U.S. Supreme Court's decision legalizing most abortions. In any event, he said, _the fetus never was born and never legally became a person._" Reasoning like that would have got Gosnell and Hyatt off. (59)

Do I need to point out that before the emancipation proclamation That African Americans were property and not considered human? In fascist Germany the Jews were not considered human but parasites on humanity? Do you see how, once we've de-humanized a person we wind up doing the unthinkable? A human being should be under the protection of the law from the womb to the tomb. We should not be allowed to de-humanize any person simply because we don't want them or due to race, religion, creed or even orientation. Pro-lifers are right to compare the plight of the unborn to the plights of African Americans and the Jewish race.

The good doctor recently passed on to his eternal reward in 2013 he's being hailed in the media as a civil rights leader and an advocate for women's rights. (60)

Why is Dr. Edelin revered and Dr. Gosnell in prison? I wonder how many other fetuses born alive were destroyed by Edelin? I wonder how many more abortionists are doing the same thing?

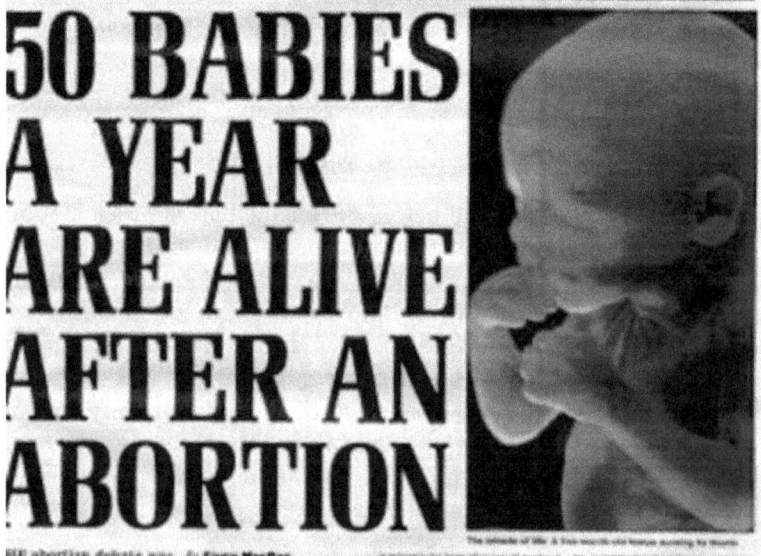

How many have been killed and how many were allowed to live their lives?

The last woman attacker I want to discuss in this chapter is the man who aborted Gianna Jessen. Dr. Edward C. Allred. As soon as I began research on this abortionist I found one review on him and his practice: Jul 21st, 2009

"What a joke that experience was! I had to go to nursing school to find out just how substandard that "care" was. Too bad women out there are still going to you...thanks for the horrible experience...and now I find out that you were an Army surgeon in Vietnam???? That explains a lot." (61)

Margaret Sanger would be so proud of Dr. Allred, you see, this racist is bent on killing as many Hispanic babies as possible. He sets up his clinics in the poorest neighborhoods. Yes, Dr. Allred owns a chain of abortion clinics in the country. It's been reported that Allred's abortion business generates $70 million per year of which he makes about $5 million. (62)

There are far more than 10-15 deaths from abortion related complications each year. As we have already discussed only 45 states report their numbers to the CDC and so many more are covered up. Some of Dr. Allred's hidden statistics include Patricia Chacon a 16-year-old Hispanic girl, Mary Peata, a 43-year-old Hispanic woman, Deanna Bell, a 13-year-old black girl, Josefina Garcia, a 37-year-old Filipino woman, Laniece Dorsey, a 17-year-old black girl and Joyce Orenzio, a 32-year-old Hawaiian woman. (63)

If it seems that the good doctor is targeting minorities it is apparantly true, as we've mentioned already, his distaste for minorities was made very clear in the doctor's own words: "Population control is too important to be stopped by some right-wing pro-life types. Take the new influx of Hispanic immigrants. Their lack of respect for democracy and social order is frightening. I hope I can do something to stem that tide; I'd set up a clinic in Mexico for free if I could . . . The survival of our society could be at stake . . . When a sullen black woman of 17 or 18 can decide to have a baby and get welfare and food stamps and become a burden to all of us it's time to stop." (64)

Now let's think about that politically for a moment. The Republicans, as a party, want to restrict abortion and abortion access while the democrats, as a party, want to stop all restrictions to abortion and make it completely legal in all states up until the day of birth (see both party platforms for more details on where each party stands on the subject.) and yet the democrats want to be perceived as the party of civil rights. They court minority votes and set themselves up as champions of the African Americans and Hispanics.

The Democrats own policies make it possible for the Allred's of this country to operate. If Hilary Clinton is elected President, then she will try to overturn the Hyde amendment (65) and make it possible for poor women to have abortions on tax payer money. This will increase the number of African American and Hispanic babies that are destroyed and keep both races as minorities. Remember, Allred said he would set up a free clinic in Mexico if he could.

The statistics do not lie: "According to 2010 census data, African Americans make up 12.6% of the U.S. population but the Centers for Disease Control (CDC) reports that black women accounted for 35.4% of all abortions in 2009. The Guttmacher Institute (AGI) puts the percentage of black abortions at 30% of the U.S. total. Their most recent numbers are from 2008. Similarly, AGI tells us that Hispanic women accounted for 25% of all U.S. abortions in 2008, though Hispanics make up just 16.3% of the U.S. population. The CDC lists the percentage of Hispanic abortions at 20.6%. Compare those numbers to non-Hispanic whites, who make up 63.7% of America's population, but account for only 36% of all U.S. abortions" (37.7% according to the CDC). (66)

So if there is a sudden increase in low income abortions then what will happen to the minorities in this country? The number of abortions will increase which means that the percentage of African Americans and Hispanics will shrink. Who are the true racists? The ones who want the number of non-whites to shrink.

I have only scratched the surface of the atrocities that are going on under our nose. The media, as we have seen, does not report on these stories, only when a sniper shoots up an abortion clinic or when someone tries to put Planned Parenthood in a bad light. Their bias is blatantly obvious. This has to turn around. I would encourage anyone who wouldn't be biased to get involved somehow in the U.S. news media and journalism. If Hilary Clinton wins the presidency she will assuredly appoint justices to the Supreme Court that will try to undo the restrictions on abortion that are in place, undermining *Casey V Reproductive Health*.

Anytime laws are passed in this country the courts overstep their boundaries and block the laws they don't like, saying that they're unconstitutional. These are not the powers that the court should have. Their job should be to interpret the laws, not strike down those they disagree with. Regardless, whoever runs the courts runs the country. Instead of a Government of the people, by the people and for the people, we've become a government of the courts, by the courts and for the courts.

That is why it is important to have the right justices appointed to the supreme court of this once great country. I cannot believe that the injustices that I've written about have gone on and are going on in this country and no one knows about it. When our soldiers liberated the Jewish people from the concentration camps in fascist Germany, the German citizens were shown films of the atrocities going on in the camps and they denied it happened. They accused the Americans of creating those films in Hollywood. They could not accept what was happening under their own noses.

I could have shown you very graphic photos of the atrocities that went on in Gosnell's office but I spared you those images. If you would like to see the full scope of what went on just type his name in your search engine and see them for yourselves. It's barbaric and inhuman.

I hope this volume has enlightened you and shown you the truth of what goes on inside an abortuary. Do more research, there are so many of these monsters out there that have no regard for human life and exploit women in the guise of civil rights. They have no more regard for their "patients" than they would for an animal. It's all in the name of making the almighty dollar. The only thing that any of us can do to try and set it right is to vote.

I leave you with this thought:

"First they came for the Socialists, and I did not speak out—
Because I was not a Socialist.

Then they came for the Trade Unionists, and I did not speak out—
Because I was not a Trade Unionist.

Then they came for the Jews, and I did not speak out—
Because I was not a Jew.

Then they came for me—and there was no one left to speak for
me." - Martin Niemöller.

If we don't speak out for those that can't speak for themselves, how
long will it be before they come for us?

"Hundreds of other survivors of abortions are speaking up, letting the world know that we ARE children, we DO deserve a chance at life & that abortion is, clearly, NOT SAFE."
—Claire Culwell
Abortion Survivor
(A Voice For Unborn Babies!)

Thursday, November 2, 1995   Los Angeles Sentinel

Family Files Abortion-Related Wrongful Death Suit

By MICHAEL DATCHER
Staff Writer

On Monday, little black boys and girls held black and white placards as tall as they were. "JUSTICE FOR THE WRONGFUL DEATH OF TA TANISHA WESSON," the signs read.

Ta Tanisha Wesson's parents, extended family and friends gathered in front of the Family Planning Associates abortion clinic to hold a press conference announcing their wrongful death suit against the clinic owner, Dr. Edward C. Allred.

Ta Tanisha Wesson's father, Lin Wesson, said, "My daughter went to this abortion clinic and never came home."

According to the Wesson's attorney, William N. McMillan III, on January 26 of this year, Ta Tanisha Wesson, 24, and a female friend, Mickey Gaton, went to the Family Planning Associates clinic located at 601 So. Westmoreland near downtown.

While Gaton sat in the waiting area, Ta Tanisha was given an abortion. Complications arose and several hours later, Gaton saw an ambulance outside the clinic and found out the person was Ta Tanisha.

Although the clinic staff knew that Gaton was with Ta Tanisha, she was not informed of the very serious complications.

Gaton called Ta Tanisha's parents, who rushed down to the clinic but were not given any information by the staff.

"Everything was done in secrecy," Lin Wesson said.

Ta Tanisha Wesson never recovered from a coma-like state. She died in the hospital leaving David, her 5-year-old son.

Family spokesperson Susan Carpenter McMillan said, gesturing to David who had a baseball cap pulled over his head, "All my words could never speak as eloquently as the expression on this little boy's face who will never see his mother again."

Attorney McMillan spoke about the details of the wrongful death suit.

"This death could have definitely been avoided. In our wrongful death suit, we are claiming that Ta Tanisha Wesson was given too much anesthesia, which caused her to vomit and choke.

"We are claiming negligence by the clinic staff who were not present when she began vomiting and ultimately delayed 20-25 minutes before calling for emergency help," McMillan said.

The attorney also stated that several abortion-related lawsuits have been filed against Allred in the past.

Dr. Edward C. Allred has a troubling approach to his abortion business and equally troubling attitudes towards African Americans.

In an article published in the San Diego Union newspaper in 1980, the doctor expressed some of his views.

"Allred and his staff work quickly. Allred likes to spend no more than five minutes on each abortion," the article states.

The San Diego Union quotes Allred, "We try to use the physician for his technical skill and reduce the one-to-one relationship with the patient ... we usually see the patient for the first time on the operating table and then not again. More contact is just not efficient."

In the same article Allred makes the following comment about African Americans, "When a sullen black woman of 17 or 18 can decide to have a baby and get welfare and food stamps and become a burden to all of us, it's time to stop. In parts of South Los Angeles having babies for welfare is the only industry the people have."

Spokesperson Susan Carpenter McMillan, who is white, said, "Since white abortionist Allred has a history of racist remarks and Ta Tanisha is African American, we question if her death was due to outrageous medical practice alone or if the fact that she is black made the clinic even

less attentive to her condition."

The Wessons want a full investigation into the matter and hope to have the clinic closed down.

An anguished Lin Wesson approached the microphone, clearly trying to be strong for his weeping wife, Nicole, standing by his side. "We are here to seek justice. Justice for our daughter Ta Tanisha Wesson. Justice is our weapon. We did not come here with guns and knives like criminals. We have come armed with the justice in our legal system. Justice is our weapon," he said.

For additional information call Gina Becker (818) 449-4834.

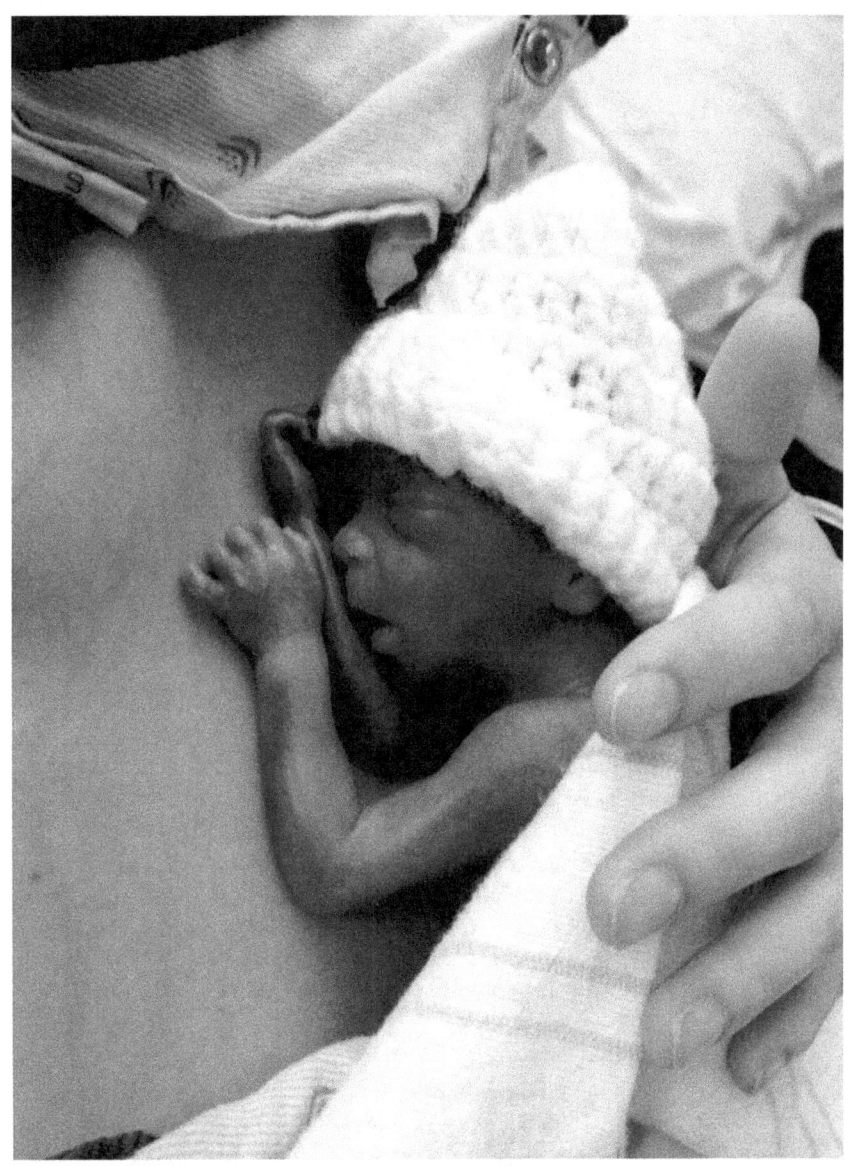

A premature baby at 22 weeks.

Bibliography:

1) Unplanned: The Dramatic True Story of a Former Planned Parenthood Leader's Eye-Opening Journey across the Life Line - by Abby Johnson, Cindy Lambert Paperback: 320 pages Publisher: Tyndale Momentum; Enlarged ed. edition (December 1, 2014) ISBN-10: 1414396546 ISBN-13: 978-1414396545

2) Blackout: The Gosnell Grand Jury Report the Media Does Not Want You to Read 1st Edition by Jonah Goldberg Paperback: 203 pages Publisher: Beaufort Books; 1 edition (May 28, 2013) ISBN-10: 0825307260 ISBN-13: 978-0825307263

3) Pro-Life Answers to Pro-Choice Arguments Expanded & Updated Paperback – November 10, 2000 by Randy Alcorn, Paperback 455 pages, publisher Multnomah ISBN-10: 1576737519, ISBN 13: 978-1576737514

4) The Walls Are Talking: Former Abortion Clinic Workers Tell Their Stories by Abby Johnson, Hardcover: 157 pages, Publisher: Ignatius Press; Sewn edition (March 20, 2016) ISBN-10: 1586177974 ISBN-13: 978-1586177973

5) Abolishing Abortion: How You Can Play a Part in Ending the Greatest Evil of Our Day Hardcover – August 18, 2015 by Frank Pavone, Hardcover: 256 pages, Publisher: Thomas Nelson (August 18, 2015) ISBN-10: 1400205727 ISBN-13: 978-1400205721

6) Persuasive Pro Life: How to Talk about Our Culture's Toughest Issue Paperback – October 1, 2014 by Trent Horn, Paperback: 335 pages Publisher: Catholic Answers Press (October 1, 2014) ISBN-10: 1941663044 ISBN-13: 978-194166304

Notes:

1)   https://en.wikipedia.org/wiki/Abortion_in_the_United _States

2)   https://en.wikipedia.org/wiki/Civil_Rights_Act_of_196 4

3)   http://www.lifenews.com/2015/03/06/7-early-feminist-leaders-here-were-pro-life-on-abortion/

4)   https://en.wikipedia.org/wiki/Feminists_for_Life

5)   https://rewire.news/article/2016/08/22/timeline-donald-trumps-shifting-position-abortion-rights/

6)   http://www.lifenews.com/2015/09/01/10-times-hillary-clinton-revealed-how-extreme-she-is-on-abortion/

7)   https://berkleycenter.georgetown.edu/quotes/hillary-clinton-on-the-origins-of-life-and-abortion-at-the-compassion-forum

8)   http://civilliberty.about.com/od/abortion/tp/choice_qu otes.htm

9)   http://www.breitbart.com/video/2016/04/03/hillary-clinton-unborn-person-doesnt-constitutional-rights/

10)   http://www.ontheissues.org/2016/Hillary_Clinton_Abo rtion.htm

11)   http://medical-dictionary.thefreedictionary.com/fetus

12)   https://en.wikipedia.org/wiki/Planned_Parenthood_v._
Casey

13)   https://en.wikipedia.org/wiki/Andrea_Dworkin

14)   https://en.wikipedia.org/wiki/Backlash:_The_Undeclar
ed_War_Against_American_Women

15)   https://en.wikipedia.org/wiki/Tanya_Melich

16)   https://en.wikipedia.org/wiki/Zed_Books

17)   https://en.wikipedia.org/wiki/The_Feminist_Press

18)   http://www.usnews.com/debate-club/is-there-a-
republican-war-on-women/reproductive-health-laws-prove-
gop-war-on-women-is-no-fiction

19)   http://www.webparish.com/pdfs/Late%20Ab%20and%
20Complications.pdf

20)   http://www.abortionfacts.com/stories/amy

21) https://www.amazon.com/Gianna-Aborted-Lived-About-
Living/dp/1561797111

22) http://www.giannajessen.com/about.html

23) http://groups.csail.mit.edu/mac/users/rauch/nvp/consist
ent/hentoff_nonperson.html

24) http://www.prolife.com/SARAH2.html
25) http://www.prolifeinfo.ie/abortion-
facts/survivors/ximena-renaerts/

26) http://www.tracts.com/Abortionsurvivorstory.pdf

27) http://www.culturallegacy.org/heidi-huffman

28) http://www.priestsforlife.org/testimonies/1150-i-was-a-survivor-of-abortion-i-can-remain-silent-no-more

29) http://realchoice.0catch.com/library/weekly/aa040103a.htm

30) https://www.amazon.com/Rosie-investigation-wrongful-Ellen-Frankfort/product-reviews/0803775040/ref=dp_db_cm_cr_acr_txt?ie=UTF8&showViewpoints=1

31) https://en.wikipedia.org/wiki/Penicillin#Discovery

32) http://www.abort73.com/end_abortion/what_about_illegal_abortions/

33) https://en.wikipedia.org/wiki/Gerri_Santoro

34) http://clinicquotes.com/wp-content/uploads/2012/08/MaternalMortality1.png

35) http://clinicquotes.com/wp-content/uploads/2012/08/MaternalMortality1.png

36) http://www.newsmax.com/DrAlvedaCKing/abortion-priests-for-life/2016/08/26/id/745395/

37) http://www.lifenews.com/2016/01/22/women-are-dying-form-legalized-abortions-but-the-mainstream-media-will-never-tell-you-about-it/

38) http://www.lifenews.com/2014/05/30/medical-examiner-confirms-woman-died-from-botched-abortion-at-cleveland-abortion-clinic/

39) http://www.wsj.com/articles/planned-parenthoods-harvest-1438211973

40) http://www.lifenews.com/2016/04/14/abortion-clinic-killed-this-woman-in-a-botched-abortion-then-her-organs-were-harvested/

41) https://en.wikipedia.org/wiki/Coma_(1978_film)

42) http://realchoice.ocatch.com/library/weekly/aa022003a.htm

43) http://abortionpillrisks.org/health-risks/deaths/#ma-deaths-us-sepsis-sordellii

44) http://afterabortion.org/2013/women-who-died-from-lifesaving-abortions/

45) *W. Phila abortion doctor had problems 38 years ago". Philadelphia Inquirer. February 4, 2011.*

46) *Taranto, James (April 18, 2013), "Back-Alley Abortion Never Ended", The Wall Street Journal.*

47) http://www.nationalreview.com/article/432405/abortion-poison-rule-roe

48) https://en.wikipedia.org/wiki/Kermit_Gosnell

49) http://www.hollywoodreporter.com/news/abortion-doctor-kermit-gosnell-tv-702666

50) http://www.imdb.com/title/tt3722234/

51) https://en.wikipedia.org/wiki/Andrew_Klavan

52) https://www.indiegogo.com/projects/gosnell-movie/#/

53) http://www.nytimes.com/1991/12/05/nyregion/doctor-describes-death-of-a-girl-who-suffered-botched-abortion.html

54) http://realchoice.ocatch.com/library/deaths/bl90smccoy.htm

55) http://www.nytimes.com/1991/11/21/nyregion/7-more-patients-accuse-doctor-of-botching-their-abortions.html?pagewanted=print&src=pm

56) http://www.nytimes.com/1993/06/15/nyregion/prison-term-for-doctor-convicted-in-abortions.html

57) http://www.thecrimson.com/article/1975/1/10/testimony-begins-this-morning-in-edelin/

58) http://www.theatlantic.com/past/docs/issues/95sep/abortion/myda.htm

59) http://www.theatlantic.com/past/docs/issues/95sep/abortion/myda.htm

60) https://www.bostonglobe.com/metro/obituaries/2013/12/31/kenneth-edelin-advocate-for-women-health-care-his-manslaughter-conviction-abortion-case-was-overturned/R4wxQ3deRTwbeD0P7UMA2L/story.html

61) http://www.vitals.com/doctors/Dr_Edward_Allred/reviews#ixzz4K71pa5iG

62) http://www.lifeissues.org/radio/r2002/03/r2798.html

63) http://afterabortion.org/2000/the-cover-up-why-u-s-abortion-mortality-statistics-are-meaningless/

64) "Doctor's Abortion Business Is Lucrative", *San Diego Union*, Oct. 12, 1980 B1:1.

65) http://www.slate.com/blogs/xx_factor/2016/01/11/why_hillary_clinton_s_call_out_of_the_hyde_amendment_is_so_important.html

66) http://www.abort73.com/abortion/abortion_and_race/

h